CO-BPZ-909

The Mutilating God

The Mutilating God

Authorship and Authority in the Narrative of Conversion

Gerald Peters

The University of Massachusetts Press / Amherst

Printed in the United States of America
LC 93–22151
ISBN 0–87023–891–4
Designed by Susan Bishop
Printed and bound by Thomson-Shore, Inc.

Library of Congress Cataloging-in-Publication Data
Peters, Gerald, 1952–
The mutilating God : authorship and authority in the narrative of conversion / Gerald Peters.
p. cm.
Includes bibliographical references and index.
ISBN 0–87023–891–4 (alk. paper)
1. Narration (Rhetoric)—Psychological aspects.
2. Autobiography—Authorship. 3. Conversion in literature. 4. Identity (Psychology) in literature.
5. Authority in literature. 6. Literature, Modern—History and criticism. I. Title.
PN212.P48 1993
809′.93592—dc20 93–22151

British Library Cataloguing in Publication data are available.

This book is published with the support and cooperation of the University of Massachusetts at Boston.

For my parents

Contents

Acknowledgments

Initial research for this book was facilitated by a fellowship from the Social Sciences and Humanities Research Council of Canada. The final process of revision and rewriting was expedited by a University of Southern Maine Summer Faculty Fellowship. A short section in Chapter 6 first appeared in an article in *The Maine Scholar* 2 (Autumn 1989). An earlier version of Chapter 7 originally appeared in *MOSAIC* 25, no. 1 (Winter 1992).

I wish to thank Michael Palencia-Roth for his encouragement and insightful criticism throughout the process of writing this work. More than anyone I know, Michael has understood the importance of maintaining a personal investment in the often rarefied activity of scholarship. I am also grateful to F. C. McGrath for his careful reading of the manuscript when it was nearly completed and for the two afternoon fishing expeditions from which I returned richer in helpful suggestions for revision than in fish.

I thank my children, Sarah, Katherine, Michael, and Ryan, for bringing such joy and meaning to my life. I owe my deepest gratitude and appreciation to my friend and partner, Anita, without whom this book could not have been written.

The Mutilating God

Introduction

> In order to write prose one must delve deeply into oneself. . . . Prose has to be built like a cathedral; there one is truly without name, without ambition, without help: on the scaffolding and alone with one's conscience. — Rilke, *Briefe 1907–1914* 63

RAISED IN AN Anabaptist family, I learned early on the necessary connection between ideology and identity. In the Anabaptist community, it is not enough to be born with a particular cultural and religious heritage. To acquire the right to this heritage one must become conscious of its social, political, and historical ramifications, then decide either to accept its mandates and restraints or to reject them in favor of another way of life. There is no middle road. In its pure form, the Anabaptist choice is a radical one, even antinomian in character, involving complete freedom of will and a total acceptance of individual responsibility for one's conduct. Quite a tall order for an eighteen-year-old, which is generally the age when young people raised as I was decide whether or not to commit themselves to the Anabaptist way of life. Perhaps not surprisingly, I found that most of my peers quite cheerfully underwent this initiatory process after the requisite period of soul-searching. I was among those who did not.

I like to think it was this early choice, fruit of the existential anguish of an eighteen-year-old, that led me to literature. At all events it is quite likely the seriousness with which this decision was treated, both by myself and others, that turned my passion for reading into a serious quest. For who was I now? How could I justify myself? In what way could I exist outside the social and linguistic sphere that I had rejected? Then again, did it really make any difference whether I was inside or outside of the lifeboat, supported by the community or swimming (as it seemed then) on my own? Literature offered me a life preserver, and I clung to it with the tenacity of a man who believes he would otherwise drown. Buoyed by my imagination and provisioned by a seemingly endless quantity of books, I set out on a quest that not only eventually gave me my livelihood but also transformed my life. The following chapters tell the story of that quest through literature. One might consider the work something on the order of a critical autobiography—an apologia defending my rejection of a specific religious ideology but also an allegory of personal development, a bildungsroman whose adventures consist of a series of formative encounters with literature. As it turned out, this quest was not the solitary and heroic undertaking I had initially envisioned but the obligatory journey into culture, an initiation open to anyone eager to understand the relation between individual identity and the traditions in language which make the construction of this identity possible.

My intention was to analyze the very strategy of self-conception that I had rejected, to determine its sources, identify its variants. In my own experience, this strategy took on the structure of a "conversion narrative." One simply underwent a conversion at the appropriate time, after which one understood the rightness of one's commitments. What surprised me was the prevalence of this type of narrative in Western literature. Wherever it appeared, it generally fulfilled the same totalizing function, offering a means of creating a unified conception of individual identity legitimized by a prevailing or emerging form of social authority. The end effect was both liberating and subjugating. It tied one to the authority of a social and linguistic context, and yet it transferred all the authority of that context to the individual in his or her dealings with the world. Such a self-conception offered the individual protection from various threats (real or imaginary) and a liberating sense of assurance: it promised, in effect, personal "salvation."

In Western literature the ideas of salvation and conversion traditionally have been associated with Christianity, beginning in the New Testament with conversions like that of St. Paul and continued in later confessional writings like Augustine's *Confessions*, Dante's *La vita nuova*, Bunyan's *Grace Abounding* . . . , Carlyle's *Sartor Resartus*, and Newman's *Apologia pro vita sua.* According to A. D. Nock's classic study of the subject, religious conversions such as these involve "a reorientation of the soul of an individual, his deliberate turning from indifference or from an earlier form of piety, a turning which implies a consciousness that a great change is involved, that the old was wrong and the new is right" (7). William James provides a more psychological explanation when he defines conversion as "the process, gradual or sudden, by which a self, hitherto divided, and consciously wrong, inferior and unhappy, becomes consciously right, superior and happy, in consequence of its firmer hold upon religious realities" (189). These two definitions furnish us with two critically distinct conceptions of the idea. Nock's assessment of conversion as a reorientation of the soul comes directly from the Greek *epistrophē*, the word coined by Plato as the goal of a philosophical education and the term adopted by early Christians for conversion. (In its most radical form the concept of epistrophe also relates to the Jungian term *enantiodromia*, or "conversion into its opposite.") James's emphasis on conversion as a psychological process of synthesis redefines the traditional metaphysical concept in terms of an internal phenomenon by grounding it in the modern metaphysics of self. Side by side, these two viewpoints abridge an entire history of human striving for self-understanding, the "evolution from religion to modern psychology" which Otto Rank has argued is "nothing but a progressive individualization of spiritual belief which gradually turned from the universal soul to the individual soul or ego" (11). Whether one describes the process of conversion as the reorientation of a sick soul or the synthesis of a divided self, the goal undoubtedly remains the same—personal salvation, preservation from harm, deliverance from evil—in essence, the liberation of the individual from some sort of unhappy state.

The question What must I do to be saved? need not be restricted to the Christian world. Nock's definition of conversion as a reorientation of the soul, a movement from indifference or from one set of beliefs to another could apply in all manner of cultural contexts. Moreover, since beliefs are grounded in collective agreement, a conversion experience has a social dimension and implies the initiation of the individual into a group and his or her adoption of the norms and practices advocated by the group. This holds true as much for primitive initiation rites with their dramatized ceremonies of rebirth as it does for initiation by baptism in early Christian communities. The initiatory aspect of conversion is also a crucial ingredient of modern social organization and finds its most fitting literary expression in the ideological novel, or *roman à thèse*, whose sole purpose is to convert the reader to some fixed political or religious ideology. According to Susan Suleiman, such "authoritarian fictions" are often patterned after the conversion narrative, indicating the individual's paradoxical need for authority in order to be liberated.

Many recent critics of autobiography have remarked upon the

fact that conversions are prevalent in secular autobiographies and may well be an integral part of the structure and goals of the genre itself. Georges Gusdorf, a pioneer in the contemporary critical conquest of autobiography as a literary genre, asserts that "the task of autobiography is first of all a task of personal salvation" (39). Stephen Shapiro's exploration of the "dark continent of literature" reveals the "structural metaphor" of conversion, or the "turning point," to be "one of the most important conventions" in autobiography (439). According to Shapiro, the motive for writing autobiography is "identity formation," the process of integrating the present self with earlier versions of the self (445). Karl J. Weintraub also links autobiographical writing with a quest for personal salvation and offers a practical explanation for the popularity of the convention of a conversion narrative:

> The genuine autobiographical effort is guided by a desire to discern and to assign meaning to a life. This effort is usually dominated by a writer's "point of view," in the most literal sense of the coordinate point in space and time at which the autobiographer stands to view his life. The essential issue is that such a point in time is located on the lifeline of a writer somewhere beyond a moment of crisis or beyond an experience, or a cumulative set of experiences which can play the same function as a crisis. This aspect comes forcefully to the fore in that type of autobiography which is built around a "conversion" experience. (824)

To this explanation we may add the allusion to conversion by James Olney, who refers to the difficulty of obtaining a vision of completeness and harmony in autobiography unless by "recording the death of the old individual—the Old Adam—and laying that individual to rest within the confines of the conversion narrative" ("Autobiography" 25).

The fact that these and other contemporary critics uphold the conversion, or turning point, as an important convention in secular autobiography, and personal salvation as a central motive for writing one, indicates a need for more detailed analysis of the subject. The evidence that the structures of many modern secular autobiographies follow a similar pattern of loss and compensatory gain found in earlier religious confessions suggests in itself grounds for a comparison and for tentatively carrying over the language of religion into the secularized quest for identity and justification. John N. Morris has given us an early example of this kind of comparison in his *Versions of the Self*, which identifies a selection of nineteenth-century autobiographies with earlier religious confessions. However, although Morris makes the structural connection between religious and secular narratives of self, he does not examine the different, often contradictory functions of the conversion narrative in various secular texts. Implicit in his study, moreover, is the tendency to naturalize the *idea* of conversion, thus conferring a kind of reverse legitimacy on the originary religious narrative. As I will show in my overview in chapter 1, the idea of conversion as an ideological tool goes back at least as far as the Greek philosophical schools, just as its pattern can be found in initiation practices of earlier societies. We might be warned at the outset, therefore, that my use of the term "conversion narrative" might seem somewhat misleading, since it implies a Christian origin rather than denoting a variety of historical applications of a narrative structure. I have used the term because it has such a familiar profile in our culture. Nevertheless, despite the centrality of this totalizing narrative, its naturalization is a mystification of linguistic convention. All conventions, however embedded in cultural practice, are subject to new uses, mutations, even extinction. In the following chapters I want to extend the horizon of my comparison of this narrative practice by tracing major structural features of the conversion narrative from primitive rituals of initiation through both classical and Christian traditions to poetic versions in modern literature. To this end I have chosen works by St. Augustine, Michel de Montaigne, the Marquis de Sade, Jean-Jacques Rousseau, Thomas De Quincey, Thomas Carlyle, James Joyce, Franz Kafka, Rainer Maria Rilke, and George Orwell. The diversity of my selection in itself should suggest that this study is not meant to be a history of the *idea* of conversion. Instead, it is intended to be a genealogy of the *uses* of this totalizing narrative in linking individual identity to various forms of social authority.

Anyone interested in the study of the conversion narrative as a religious genre will find among several standard works on the subject an excellent example of current scholarship done in the field in Karl F. Morrison's investigations of the idea of conversion in medieval Europe. Unlike my own aims, which are both more speculative and more limited, Morrison resolves to "enter into the minds of people in a distant age and, by a kind of archaeology, to reconstruct their hermeneutics of conversion" (*Understanding Conversion* xii). By contrast, I wish to bracket the notion of conversion as an idea or presence that permeates the religious tradition to which it must belong. I intend to show that a narrative has a life of its own and can be deployed in a wide variety of contexts, even those which subvert the very traditions from which it derives. Nevertheless, while the migration of a narrative form does not ensure a continuity of content, it does effect a kind of transference of its authorizing power. Winston Smith's conversion to totalitarianism in *Nineteen Eighty-Four*, while figurally and structurally recapitulating Augustine's conversion, is by no means a representation of the same experience, but it is equally as significant a representation of experience for its time. Similarly, the inclusion of a satiric deathbed conversion scene from the Marquis de Sade may seem somewhat unsettling to anyone expecting a history of the idea of conversion, but it captures the emergence of secular materialism in Europe in a way that a traditional religious narrative of the period could only counter. As my genealogy of writing practices suggests, conversion narratives have been used in the most disparate and contradictory ways. What is intriguing to me is not how the formula is strictly adhered to and repeated but, rather, how it is renovated, adapted, and deployed.

A historical review of significant self-representational texts reveals how the conversion narrative has become less and less of a liberating strategy, as if it were a narrative practice that needed to be overcome. The resistance to totalizing strategies in narrative becomes quite evident in twentieth-century literature, where the conversion narrative is often treated with ambiguity or even as an obstacle to identity formation. My readings of Joyce's *Portrait of the Artist as a Young Man*, Rilke's *Notebook of Malte Laurids Brigge*, and Orwell's *Nineteen Eighty-Four* reveal the extent to which Western conceptions of identity are informed by this totalizing narrative and the difficulty of representing alternatives to its limiting power.

In order to relate these modern texts to earlier modes of self-representation, however, I think it is necessary to account for the fact that language has not been used in the same way in every period but has undergone fundamental transformations which reflect (and shape) the way people conceive of the world and of themselves.

Northrop Frye has given us an example of such an approach when he employs an expanded version of Vico's theory of the history of writing in order to show how the language of the Bible has been taken up by succeeding epochs in Western literature. Following Vico, Frye sees three major phases in the development of writing: a hieroglyphic, or "metaphoric," phase, which includes all forms of verbal expression that precede Plato; a hieratic, or "logocentric," phase, made possible by the new modes of organization in writing beginning with Plato; and a demotic, or "descriptive," phase, which emerges in the sixteenth century and which comes to ascendancy by the end of the eighteenth century as a result of developing notions of rationalism and empiricism.

To be sure, my brief survey should not be taken as a proof of Frye's concepts. Stronger support for such developments in language use can be found, for example, in Alexander Luria's rationalist study of the development of language, or in Julian Jaynes's ambitious, albeit highly speculative, work on the history of consciousness. Thus, what Frye describes as the metaphoric phase of language use reflects Luria's more pragmatic socialist conception of the "sympractical" nature of language in its early development. In both Frye's and Luria's conceptions of this early stage in the phylogenesis of language, words are "concrete" and intensely physical. Little distinction is possible between a subject and an object. People live in language the way we live in dreams—unreflectively, unconsciously, experiencing every image as a poetic and "magical" reality. Indeed, this is the position from which Julian Jaynes is able to assert that before the fourth or fifth century B.C., people *were* unconscious, ordering their existences on the basis of hallucinatory directives that came from their "bicameral" minds.

Frye makes no such exotic claims. He is only categorizing the characteristic changes taking place in central texts of each period. Thus, Frye's "hieratic phase" begins with Plato, somewhat after Jaynes situates the emergence of consciousness. But the essential characteristics of Plato's revolutionary new use of language are precisely those which Jaynes argues are necessary to produce the interior space in which to "visualize" the subjective "analogue" I, the prerequisite for conscious reflection. As Frye points out, the hieratic phase is characterized by a "more individualized" use of language in which words "primarily express inner thoughts or ideas" (7). If metaphor characterizes the earlier conception of language, the hieratic mode is dominated by the concept of metonymy. Words are "put for" thoughts—they are "outward expressions of an inner reality" (7). This understanding of words as signs for ideas enables the writer to make sharper, more consistent distinctions between subject and object. "Reflection," says Frye, "with its overtones of looking into a mirror, moves into the verbal foreground" (7). Moreover, intellect and emotion become perceived as separate operations of the mind, making possible the concepts of logic and abstract thinking. Not only are words the outward expression of an inner reality, they are tokens of an ideal, transcendent order, allowing an integrated and unified system of consciousness, a system which necessitates a central premise or a monotheistic universe around which all thoughts can be organized. According to Frye, the hieratic phase must be identified with the emergence of continuous prose writing with its superior ability to mediate between and unify the disparate representations of the poetic consciousness of the earlier phase.

Frye's final category of writing, the demotic phase, emerges in the sixteenth century and comes to ascendancy by the end of the eighteenth century. In this mode of writing language no longer works deductively from single premises (either analogically or allegorically) but functions in an inductive and descriptive fashion. Words are not to be subsumed by a transcendental order but must faithfully reflect what they describe. "The ideal to be achieved by words," Frye tells us, "is framed on the model of truth by correspondence" (13). The dominant figure of speech, then, is not metaphor or metonymy but simile, that is, "a true verbal structure is one that is *like* what it describes" (13). This relation, Frye points out, resembles the relation of words to nature in the metaphoric phase, but with one important difference. The subject is for the first time completely distinguished from an "objective" world. By implying an ideal subjectivity constructed on the model of an extended, rational, and deductive system of notation, the idea of objectivity offers the means by which the transcendental perspective of the hieratic phase can be undermined. Thus, Frye concludes, "Extreme forms of third-phase thinking, demonstrate the 'impossibility of metaphysics,' or declare that all religious questions are unmeaning" (13).

The following chapters set forth a genealogy of writing practices which corresponds to these categories, outlining how the idea of conversion has become an increasingly internalized phenomenon through a conception of self and world that is more and more differentiated. Thus, in the primitive world, the concept of conversion is tied completely to the magical transformations of the human body through rites of initiation. In later monotheistic or logos-centered societies these ritualized activities become transformed into the narrative patterns and metaphors that link individual identity with metaphysically grounded forms of social unity and power. In the modern world the narrative of conversion becomes both a means by which individualized identities undermine traditional forms of authority and a means by which conflicting ideological communities attempt to impose their orders on individuals through methods of indoctrination and coercion. This, then, is the itinerary which my selection of texts seeks to elaborate and confirm.

If we are to accept the utility of Frye's elaboration of Vico's theory of writing, we must be careful not to apply their categories too rigidly. Frye's predominantly formalist orientation tends to present language as undergoing a kind of isolated evolution, cut off from social, political, and economic forces which motivate and complicate the very changes he describes. Moreover, Frye's at times too generous formulation of categories does not account for more recent claims that language is fraught with internal tensions—conflicts which have been identified in the "anti-elitist" tradition of the carnival and, as I will show in chapter 5, in the hermetic tradition. Frye's preoccupation with archetypal patterns should not, however, be set in direct opposition to a "historical" approach to literature. Indeed, Frye's attempt to create a properly structural understanding of "Literature" in some ways paved the way for a text-based historical analysis. For all its sophistication, however, one of the central problems of Frye's approach was that it reiterated the monolithic model of the day, which identified itself almost solely with the cultural elite. Nevertheless, properly contextualized, Frye's affiliation with an elitist critical tradition need not be seen as a drawback. As I intend to show, moreover, the very tradition of conversion, so bound up with the hegemonic continuance of the patriarchy, typically involves a social operation designed to induct the individual into a prevailing sociopolitical power structure. To trace the uses of the totalizing narrative of conversion is to some extent to follow the vicissitudes of the language of power.

Finally, we should not attribute to Frye's evolutionary model oversimplified notions of progress. Language is fundamentally conservative, utilizing and adapting the very master narratives and constituent figures of the modes of understanding that it is intent on replacing, putting them to new uses or preserving them in such a way that they do not appear to interfere significantly with the employment of new strategies. We have long been aware, however, that such "interference" persists in language—indeed, that language seems to operate to a great extent on the basis of this interference. The conflict between modes of discourse at specific times in history may well lie at the very root of the division of knowledge into various disciplines. Thus, as the conquest of the external environment required a more objectifying language, it became necessary to develop strategies to frame each mode to keep it from either interfering with or being completely undermined by emerging modes of thought. It would only stand to reason, however, that at any given time, one form of discourse would be considered more prestigious or important than another and would hold other forms hostage to its influence. Indeed, the very structure and hierarchy of these divisions becomes the overarching hermeneutic by which we are forced to interpret our affairs.

I would argue, therefore, that we must not see the demotic phase as the ultimate goal but as a dominant and ongoing mode of understanding, a further complication in the development of our relation to language. In an important sense Frye's three categories of language use exist simultaneously in our own speech, representing conflicting ways in which we define and experience time and space. An evolutionary model of language use therefore merely describes the successive privileging of one concept of time/space over another in history, reflecting the dominant usage in any given period. A purely demotic use of language is, of course, impossible. The relativity of even the most demotic language has been understood at least since the ground-breaking work of Ferdinand de Saussure, who saw a necessary separation between a signifier and what it signified. According to Saussure, meanings could be produced in language only through its internal operations and not through identity with some fundamental meaning or reality outside of itself. Saussure's observations have provided one of the bases for the contemporary challenge to the metaphysical presuppositions underlying all modes of Western discourse. The demotic phase would be only the most recent version of these presuppositions: a purely descriptive, "scientific" language (i.e. a language in which words are believed to be *like* what they describe) would not necessarily escape what Jacques Derrida refers to as the "logocentric enclosure" of a "metaphysics of presence."

By accounting, however provisionally, for the fact that words are not used in the same way in different historical settings, we address one of the difficulties in comparing ancient and modern epistemologies. In so doing, we also annul the position of privilege given to the notion of a unified, de facto subject determined in a causal way by a chronological series of objectifiable "events." This position becomes one of several versions of self, each a product of the dominant mode of understanding. We must begin with a premise that the self is a fiction, a mirage produced by the specific effects of language. This is nothing new. The notion of a permanent, unified self was already called into question by David Hume, who argued that a unifying center of consciousness is impossible to verify either logically or descriptively. And, as Paul Jay points out, the "notion that the self exists as a unified and pure spirit" was also criticized by Nietzsche as nothing more than a tradition in Western writing that had no ontological status prior to its "purely discursive origins" (28). Jay argues that the notion of a fixed and permanent self falls into jeopardy during the Romantic period in texts like Wordsworth's *Prelude*, suffers a singular defeat in the ironic perambulations of Carlyle's *Sartor Resartus*, undergoes a fictional revival in Joyce's *Portrait*, and is eventually abandoned altogether in works like Henry Adams's *Education* and Roland Barthes's *Roland Barthes*. The question remains, however, given that the acceptance of a unified self is historically determined, Why do such totalizing conventions as the conversion narrative persist? Jay implicitly recognizes this situation when he argues that although texts like *Roland Barthes by Roland Barthes* may show us the limits or even the impossibility of "self-writing," they do not augur the end of autobiography itself (327). "People will no doubt continue to write quite traditional [autobiographies]" he concludes, although he does not speculate as to why this may be so.

There is good reason why the conversion narrative has remained embedded in self-writing, despite shifting epistemologies. The knowledge that the "unified self" is only an illusion produced by conventions in writing does not, in itself, eliminate the psychological need or the social imperative to understand oneself as a totality. Lacanian psychoanalytic theory, for example, equates the primary idea of the self with a prelinguistic imago of the human body and raises what it calls the fragmented body to the level of a fundamental psychological category. Thus, according to Lacan, the fear of fragmentation is more fundamental than the fear of death itself. The persistence of totalizing strategies in narrative might therefore be understood in terms of their restorative function at a prerational level. This, moreover, is where Lacan's categories of the imaginary and the symbolic intersect, since a unity of subjectivity also appears to be a necessary condition for participation within the sociosymbolic contract.

To assert this is not the same thing, however, as "naturalizing" the strategy of conversion. Certainly there are other means of creating satisfyingly unified conceptions of identity in language. Moreover, some may argue that the notion of a unity of subjectivity is no longer really a necessary part of a postmodern identity, an assertion which I think must be taken seriously and which demands further investigation. To be sure, many contemporary autobiographers attempt to interrupt and undermine the illusion of a unified self. Yet there are difficulties with the assumption that fragmentation in itself heralds some kind of development or even sounds the death knell of autobiography. It might be more accurate to understand the tendency toward so-called fragmentation as part of an ongoing problem in our relation to authorizing discourses, since such a tendency relies on the very totality it undermines in order to produce its own meaning. Indeed, it may be part of a strategy of retaliation against an authorizing structure which legitimizes an unsatisfactory totality, a reaction which in its very assertiveness reveals both the dissatisfaction of not being included and the longing for a unity that has not yet come into being. Or, it may reflect only our blind faith in the demotic discourse of science, which ultimately cannot legitimize a unifying center of consciousness.

The fact that the "unified self" may be only an epistemological convention does not, however, detract from its potentially therapeutic value. Paul de Man, like many of his contemporaries, agrees that autobiography is indeed a "discourse of self-restoration" (74). But he inverts the traditional notion of autobiography as a representation of a preexisting self, arguing that "the autobiographical project may itself produce and determine the life" of the individual (69). The question posed is whether the "illusion of reference [is] not a correlation of the structure of the figure [of autobiography], that is, no longer clearly and simply a referent at all but something more akin to a fiction which then, however, in its own turn, acquires a degree of referential productivity" (69). Thus, whether the self is conceived as ontological fact or rhetorical invention would seem to be less important than the writer's recognition of the self's life-giving, unifying value. De Man concludes that autobiography is not a genre or a mode at all but a "figure of reading or of understanding that occurs, to some degree, in all texts." "The autobiographical moment," he argues, "happens as an alignment between two subjects involved in the process of reading in which they determine each other by mutually reflexive substitution" (70).

Despite various productive theoretical perspectives developed in autobiography scholarship over the past two decades, there seems to be a persistent and influential tendency in the field to remain concentrated on the referential character of autobiography and the levels of sociopolitical agreement this notion entails (Lejeune, Eakin). Although I do not disavow the value of this work, I have opted to follow de Man's approach because I believe it more accurately reflects both the range and the limits of representability in language and because it better describes the effective function of the conversion narrative in self-writing. Having thereby set aside the perhaps more ambitious questions of referentiality and genre definition, I argue for a more expansive understanding of the rhetorical figure of confession, one that not only encompasses traditionally and generically autobiographical texts but, as in the case of Orwell, even straightforward novelistic prose. In fleshing out de Man's largely theoretical conception of the autobiographical figure, moreover, I want to demonstrate how reading autobiographically constitutes a significant source of interpretive energy for the continued pursuit of "self-explication."

De Man's emphasis on autobiography as a figure of reading finds fuller expression in Janet Varner Gunn's *Poetics of Experience*. Like de Man, Gunn argues that the central concern in autobiography is not the writer but the reader. Indeed, Gunn goes even further than de Man when she states that genre itself is "first of all an instrument of reading, not primarily a formula for writing" (23). For Gunn, the autobiographical text provides a "theater for displaying ourselves to one another" and, what is more important, to ourselves. According to Gunn, the reader is a "position" in the text which must be occupied first and foremost by the writer. This self-reading takes two forms, becoming an "occasion of discovery" and an occasion for "distantiation" (19). On the one hand, the reader discovers new possibilities of selfhood through interpretation of his or her disclosures in an "activity that risks display" (20). On the other hand, by writing for a reader, writers are able to view their text from a position other than themselves—they experience "the otherness of the text" (20)—helping them to align their perspective with the world of common experience. Thus, Gunn concludes, "the autobiographical response" contains both a "hermeneutics" and a "poetics . . . bringing them into a new relation which [she calls] 'the stereoscope of readership.'"

Both de Man's and Gunn's approaches to autobiography as a dialectical discourse representing the often irremediable tension between a writing and a reading self find confirmation in the work of Jacques Lacan and his "return to Freud." To be sure, Gunn eschews overt connections to a psychological approach, rightly claiming that it too often leads to a "psychologizing of literature," the turning of a literary text into a "behavioristic model to which response can be quantified, measured and even predicted" (19). Nevertheless, psychoanalytic theory, and Lacanian *discours* in particular, can shed a great deal of light on intersubjectivity within the realm of reading. The danger, if it can indeed be interpreted as such, is that a literary text becomes the "pretext" to the theoretical discourse, particularly when the prose of that discourse is as difficult and oblique as Lacan's. In an autobiographical reading of self-representational texts, however, Freud and Lacan become central to the interpretive equation.

Psychoanalysis is especially well suited as a third term in the comparison of religious confession with other kinds of self-writing because it is itself a modern demotic paradigm of the confessional situation. Like the traditional confessor, the analyst assimilates the life history of his or her patients and attempts to liberate them from the tyranny of their past. The psychoanalytic "cure," not unlike the experience of conversion, is the turning point in which patients exchange their discontinuous history for a continuous one and try to create a unified image of self out of a formerly fragmented one. In this process, the psychoanalyst, like the confessor, performs the rite of absolution by assuming the burden of the patients' guilts and torments and, at least in theory, effects a cure.

Although Freud criticized religion and metaphysics of any kind as "a nuisance, an abuse of thinking," he also referred to the psychoanalytic program in curiously mystical and salvationist terms. In a famous passage, speaking of his model of the psyche, with its various topographical dimensions, he remarks:

> It is easy to imagine, too that certain mystical practices may succeed in upsetting the normal relations between different regions of the mind, so that, for instance, perception may be able to grasp happenings in the depths of the ego and in the id which were otherwise inaccessible to it. It may safely be doubted, however, whether this road will lead us to the ultimate truths from which salvation is to be expected. Nevertheless, it may be admitted that the therapeutic efforts of psychoanalysis *have chosen a similar line of approach* [my italics]. Its intention is, indeed, to strengthen the ego, to make it more independent of the superego, so that it can appropriate fresh portions of the id. Where id was, there ego shall be. It is a work of culture—not unlike the draining of the Zuider Zee. ("Dissection" 79–80)

I will contend that, in his formulation of the salvational doctrine of psychoanalysis, Freud was also intimating his goal of displacing an entire metaphysical tradition with a "science" of the psyche. "Wo es war, soll *ich* werden!" (Where it [i.e., previous metaphysics] was, there *I* shall be). But it was precisely Freud's relation to science which made him fall back into the very mystification he repudiated. As Jacques Derrida and others have argued, Freud's mistake was to assume that a salvational doctrine was possible under the aegis of a purely rational science. Indeed, Freud's employment of spatial and economic metaphors in a dominantly scientific discourse, which, in effect, treated language as a pure reflection of reality, created a "metaphysics of presence" that trapped Freud within the mystifying enclosure he sought to escape.

Lacanian psychoanalysis attempts to rectify the situation by grounding psychoanalysis in a study of the effects of language rather than in a science of presence. Just as Freud shifted authority from its traditional, humanistic base with his "discovery" of the unconscious,

Lacan shifts it once again by discovering in the "talking cure" a science of the psyche based on language. As do de Man and Gunn, Lacan postulates a double dimension in every dialogue, arguing that every genuine transaction in language is possible only because of our capacity to carry out a corresponding dialogue within ourselves in a dialectical arrangement between a conscious self and a repressed "other" self. According to Lacan, this repression of a part of the self occurs in response to the recognition of "otherness" outside of the self in a process he designates as the mirror stage. Here Lacan follows in the footsteps of Hegel, who originally formulated the idea of an internal splitting of a subjective self and a "negated" other self in the following way: "Self-consciousness has before it another self-consciousness; it has come outside of itself. This has a double significance. First it has lost its own self, since it finds itself as an *other* being; secondly, it has thereby sublated that other, for it does not regard the other as essentially real but sees its own self in the other" (229). If Freud's contribution to this concept of sublation, or *Aufhebung*, was the theory of the unconscious, Lacanian *discours* adds to Freud's discovery the idea of the centrality of language in the formation and function of this mirroring division. According to Lacan, the unconscious "operates like a language." Only through language and its system of differences can an "interiorized" relation be created and sustained that will make the complex intersubjective relations of human society possible. Self-consciousness occurs because of the double function of language, because unindividuated being is "alienated into the signifying chain" and must therefore undergo a transformation into a speaking and a listening subject, a conscious and a sublated text. It is language both as a social institution and a psychological structure which makes possible, as de Man said, "the alignment of two subjects . . . by mutually reflexive substitution." Language enables us to operate as individuals within a social context precisely because it contains both an "identificatory" and a "distantiating" function.

In the act of reading autobiographically, psychoanalysis plays an especially important role because it offers an epistemology which allows for the reintroduction of the subject (the reading consciousness) into knowledge. Psychoanalytic discourse is the "grammar" by which I want to constitute myself as a reader in relation to the constructed self in the text. Within the structural possibilities that such a grammar affords, I am able to reconstruct myself in terms of the signifying strategies of another's experience. I begin to hear what I ordinarily do not hear myself saying, thus opening up the possibility for self-discovery and recovery. Moreover, if, as Gunn says, an autobiographical reading involves a "risking activity," psychoanalytic theory provides the formal mediations by which the revelatory aspects of this reading can be conveyed in a universally understood form.

There is no doubt that one can no longer get away with the old, stereotypical approach of psychoanalytic literary criticism. As Shoshana Felman puts it, literature must be seen as an authority in its own right, not as a passive subject to be analyzed or operated upon by some other authoritative body of knowledge. The juxtaposition of psychoanalysis or any other form of scientific or humanistic knowledge with literature must produce a "dialectical, mutually informing relationship" (8). Ideally, then, the critic becomes an intermediary who articulates the implications of this dialectical discourse. It cannot be denied, however, that there are also pressing motives for juxtaposing theoretical forms of authority against literary ones. What is required today is a form of authority able to *display itself* as well as generate new possibilities of interpretation. "Unlike twenty years ago," Paul Ricoeur points out, "we can no longer rest content to distinguish method and doctrine." Our methods are as much a part of the analysis as the results themselves, and " 'theory' is not a contingent addition but in fact . . . [the] very object of the humane sciences" (100). Theories, like the crystal timepieces in Goethe's *Wilhelm Meister*, not only "show us the course of the hours and minutes," but they also reveal the "combination of wheels and springs" that turn them (188). They essentially satisfy our contemporary requirements for authority and "fair play" based on the skeptical notion that knowledge, in whatever form, is at bottom a word game with pretensions to truth, the rules of which must be continually open to critique.

This skeptical attitude toward the knowable makes possible a somewhat different use of theory. By bringing together two or more highly visible conceptual or representational structures of interpretation, the critic can obtain a kind of overlapping effect which lends a corroborative power to the whole. What can be achieved by overlaying texts with a variety of systems of authority which reflect different modes of language use is the discovery of sustained patterns of operation in the human understanding insofar as the various discourses reinforce one another and, conversely, the discovery of significant deviations in the pattern where they diverge. The deviations are perhaps what interest us most. By tracing the use of a narrative form, we are better able to read these differences by determining their relative positions in a historical spiral of applications.

Religion, psychoanalysis, and literature offer the richest ground for this kind of interpretation. Fredric Jameson writes,

> For any contemporary re-evaluation of the problem of interpretation, the most vital exchange of energies inevitably takes place between the two poles of the psychoanalytic and the theological, between the rich and concrete practice of interpretation contained in the Freudian texts and dramatized in the diagnostic genius of Freud himself, and the millenary theoretical reflection on the problems and dynamics of interpretation, commentary, allegory, and multiple meanings, which, primarily organized around the central text of the Bible, is preserved in the religious tradition. (69)

In the following chapters I seek to address this "vital exchange of energies" by juxtaposing the language of religious representation against the theoretical framework of a creative and speculative psychology. Thus we have an intersection of three very different but analogous forms of authority. The scientific and necessarily reductive strategies of a language-based psychology are counterbalanced by the resonant traditions of religion, both of which enter into a dialogue with the free-playing, lifelike authority of fantasy in literature. Rather than removing criticism from the "category of life," as Gunn supposes, this corroboration of authorities can illuminate life in a truly three-dimensional way. By linking modern autobiography and the autobiographical novel with religious confessions, we are better able to grasp the historical parameters of self-representation as a product of shifting conceptions of language and authority. By incorporating a psychoanalytic and theoretical dimension, we involve the "confessional" discipline that has come to displace religious thinking, and which has dominated the imaginations of many twentieth-century writers since Kafka and Joyce. In short, we are able to trace the uses of a totalizing narrative both as it prefigures the Freudian discovery and as it passes through and becomes transformed by the Freudian register in three notable examples of twentieth-century "self-representation."

Before I go on, however, I must account for one obvious omission in this work, the fact that none of the primary texts is written by a woman. This omission can be neither completely excused by the autobiographical nature of this book nor sufficiently explained by the knowledge that the conversion narrative belongs to a Western tradition of male spiritual codes. In fact, the latter aspect makes the argument for an extensive study of the uses of the conversion narrative in women's writing all the more pressing. In her recent study of American women's conversion narratives in the nineteenth and twentieth centuries, Virginia Liesen Brereton contends that conversion narratives were more prevalent in women's devotional writing than in men's. Brereton's work reflects the necessity of recovering texts that have been marginalized by canonical exclusion or by other more deeply embedded forms of bias. Yet her work also reveals the necessity of developing a more contextualized and theoretically informed understanding of the field of self-writing. Brereton implicitly recognizes this need when she concludes with a call for a more wide-ranging investigation of "the effect of conversion language upon the rest of culture" (125). One significant dimension of this sort of investigation involves the rereading of texts which, for better or worse, have formed us and our culture. The processes of recovery and rereading must be seen as interdependent; what we learn from one activity should be applied to the other as formerly marginalized works take on formative roles in a more diversified canon. Brereton's appeal for a more comprehensive investigation of the "effect of conversion language" on culture is already being answered by more theoretically informed critics of women's autobiography. Kirsten Wasson's "Geography of Conversion: Dialogical Boundaries of Self in *The Promised Land*" (Ashley, Gilmore, Peters, *Autobiography and Postmodernism*), for example, invokes Bakhtin's dialogical theory to show how Mary Antin both embraces and resists American assimilation through the deployment of the Puritan conversion narrative.

For my own part, I wish to establish a broader cultural framework for the discussion of conversion rhetoric, although perhaps in a somewhat different way than Brereton has in mind. Not only do I aim to reread traditionally significant literary texts through the extraliterary optic of the conversion narrative, but also, reciprocally, to reread a religious tradition through formative texts that have typically been excluded from the aspirations of that tradition. I want to open up the study of the totalizing narrative of conversion in order to reveal the psychosocial dialectic at work in Western self-writing between private motivation and its desired public legitimation, between the individual as the projection of an integral subject and the collective, cultural resources that constrain and/or enable the possibility of such self-projection.

The most difficult question of all for me to answer has been my own role as reader-critic in the exegesis of the literary text. Ideally, as I mentioned before, one prefers to see oneself as a mediator between different authoritative strata. But this evades the issue of one's own authority. All too often discursive prose, and perhaps my work is no exception, tends to be an exercise in self-displacement. Multifarious other authorities are crowded into the text if only to hide one's own anxiety about authority and to prove oneself by virtue of one's association with others. This is all very well. But it disguises a fundamental experience that each reader has with literature. If we are to pursue the Hegelian/Freudian/Lacanian models of intersubjectivity to their conclusion, we must posit that the very act of reading creates a corresponding internal dialogue in ourselves by which we too are determined. By participating in the position of readership that each text calls for, we become aware of parallel internal rhythms, of inner correspondences. We feel that we "see" ourselves from a different vantage point, and at the same time, we identify possibilities for selfhood hitherto unknown. Taken at its ultimate value, criticism and the appreciation of criticism are autobiographical moments in which we discover our own potential through the structured interplay of texts and forms. We need these forms to define and to re-create ourselves. Moreover, there can be no way to deny, nor should it be denied, that our choice of interpretive strategies, our choice of what is important and what is not, and our choice of the very themes themselves reflect inner exigencies looking for a way to be projected into the world through language. My choice of autobiography as a ground for investigation almost certainly reflects my own autobiographical impulse, just as my choice of the themes of conversion and salvation reflect a corresponding need to come to grips with my own past. Our blindness, as de Man says, represents our only possibility for insight.

I must emphasize, however, that the idea of reading autobiographically should not be taken in its conventional sense of a personal encoding. The self to which I refer is a transcendental subject made present and upheld through language. I concur with Rilke, who, when asked about himself, referred to "that figure which I am building beyond myself, outside, more valid and more permanent. . . . For: Who knows who I am? I am constantly changing" (*Muzot* 154). Reading autobiographically is a means of discovering the personal in the universal, a way of recognizing one's own nature in the signifying materiality of another. It is a hermeneutical activity in de Man's sense of "mutually reflexive substitution," a way of reading that testifies to the ontological significance of a literary work in the ongoing process of understanding ourselves. At the level of religion, ideology, or social allegiance, the narrative of conversion is a cultural inscription that marks each of us in our ascent to our common identity. By exploring the various functions of this master narrative as well as significant efforts to overcome its coercive power, I want to address current social anxieties (including my own) about totalizing forms of representation and the roles they play in linking identity of self to the "deep structure" of our culture.

In short, we are here not merely to interpret texts but also to be interpreted ourselves by some of the richest and most complex articulations in literature. With these remarks, it should be evident that my use of theory or the symbolic structures of religion are not only the main critical tools of my work but also the bases for formal mediations between my own inner life and the reincarnation of another's literary self-consciousness within.

I

Authorizing Inscriptions: Prefiguring the Freudian Text

CHAPTER I

The Hieroglyphic Phase

THE RITUAL of baptism, which socially validates conversion to Christianity, combines an age-old symbolism of death and rebirth found in many primitive rituals of initiation. In the first place, submersion in water symbolizes a ritual drowning of the old self—the "old Adam," as Luther puts it (*Catechism* 135)—making way for the rebirth of the newly "converted" self, cleansed of its sins. The apostle Paul links this ritual death and birth to the crucifixion and resurrection of Christ: "Do you not know that all of us who have been baptized into Christ Jesus were baptized into his death? We were buried therefore with him by baptism into death, so that as Christ was raised from the dead by the glory of the Father, we too might walk in newness of life. For if we have been united with him in a death like his, we shall certainly be united with him in a resurrection like his" (Rom. 6:3–5). There is general agreement among scholars that Christianity likely borrowed this symbolism from the Egyptian funerary myth of Osiris. Yet given that initiatory rituals of death and rebirth can be found in almost every part of the world, one could also conjecture that such symbols arise independently in the human imagination as the most fitting language to express a binding pact between the individual and his or her culture. The variations on the theme itself certainly attest to the imaginative scope of different cultures. In the initiation ceremony of the Kikuyu of East Africa, for example, Sir James Frazer tells us that "the mother stands up with the boy crouching at her feet; she pretends to go through all the labour pains, and the boy, on being reborn, cries like a babe and is washed" (11). Other tribes enact a ritual killing of the youthful initiate and then bring him back to life (12). Emile Durkheim notes the intensely literal way in which these ceremonies are taken by the participant. "This change of state is thought of, not as a simple and regular development of preexistent germs, but as a transformation (*totius substantiae*) of the whole being. It is said that at this moment the young man dies, that the person he was ceases to exist, and that another is instantly substituted for it. He is reborn under a new form. Appropriate ceremonies are felt to bring about this death and rebirth, which are not understood in a merely symbolic sense, but are taken literally" (39).

The literalism of these ceremonies is perhaps most evidenced by the fact that they are usually accompanied by the ritual mutilation of the initiate's body. Circumcision is the most common form of initiatory mutilation, one still widely performed by Muslims and Jews as well as by Christians in North America, and one which originally accompanied baptism at any age in certain sects. Paul explicitly represents Christian baptism as a symbolic displacement of circumcision when he calls it "the circumcision made without hands, in putting off the body of the sins of the flesh by the circumcision of Christ" (Col. 2:11). Yet the controversy over this practice in Western Christian societies even today should be put into perspective, given the prevalence of this form of initiatory mutilation in a great many non-Western societies. In *The Rites of Passage* Arnold Van Gennep complains of the undue emphasis that Christian scholarship has put on the rite of circumcision, when placed alongside the vast catalog of ritual mutilations practiced in the religiomagical world:

> Cutting off the foreskin is exactly equivalent to pulling out a tooth (in Australia, etc.), to cutting off the little finger above the last joint (in South Africa), to cutting off the earlobe or perforating the earlobe or the septum, or to tattooing, scarifying, or cutting the hair in a particular fashion. The mutilated individual is removed from the common mass of humanity by a rite of separation (this is the idea behind cutting, piercing, etc.) which automatically incorporates him into a defined group; since the operation leaves ineradicable traces, the incorporation is permanent.
>
> The Jewish circumcision is in no way extraordinary: it is clearly a "sign of union" with a particular deity and a mark of membership in a single community of the faithful. Finally, if one also considers excision of the clitoris, perforation of the hymen, section of the perineum, and sub-incision, it becomes apparent that the human body has been treated like a simple piece of wood which each has cut and trimmed to suit him: that which projected has been cut off, partitions have been broken through, flat surfaces have been carved—sometimes, as among the Australians, with great imagination. Circumcision is among the simplest and least serious of all these practices. (71–72)

If we are to conclude that preliterate forms of initiation are based on ritual dramatizations rather than on writing, we must at least understand the ritual mutilation of the body as a primitive form of writing, a painful inscription—as an event, a living memory and a means of identification—which marks the transition of the individual from a childhood self to a new social self.

The notion of ritual mutilation as a form of writing is borne out by Van Gennep's theory of a liminal or neutral stage between the ritual separation from the old life with its childhood dependencies and entry into the adult social order. Although the length of this liminal phase varies from one culture to the next, it is invariably a period when individuals lose their name, identity, sex, and memory of previous existence. It is during this phase, Van Gennep explains, that the ritual inscription of the new self occurs. "The neophyte in liminality must be a *tabula rasa*, a blank slate on which is inscribed the knowledge and wisdom of the group, in those respects that pertain to the new status. The ordeals and humiliations, often of a grossly physiological character, to which neophytes are submitted represent partly a destruction of a previous status and partly a tempering of their essence in order to prepare them to cope with their new responsibilities and restrain them in advance from abusing their new privileges" (103).

It is difficult to apply the word "psychology" in its modern sense to such ritual behavior. Psyche, for the primitive initiate, appears to have been unindividuated—part of the containing world. The mind of initiates enveloped and accepted as reality a dramatic order of meanings that fused object with subject. They participated in this magical drama as a living text, reenacting the cultural codes that had been inscribed on them and in their memory in a continuous cycle of repetitions. The hieroglyphic phase, consequently, seems to have begun when writing began to be separated from a literal inscription on the human body, when the living text was replaced by another form of tabula rasa, but the writing itself retained the "intensely physical" reality within which the most elemental aspect of human consciousness functions.

In one sense we can view this transition from the primitive dramatic order to a hieroglyphic order of language as a form of liberation. It certainly freed individuals from the fiercely totalizing existence within which they were condemned to act. But the shift to writing is perhaps also the beginning of the end of a magical sense of unity and of belonging. No longer totally encompassed by the drama of his or her culture, the individual became "alienated into the signifying chain," to borrow a phrase from Lacan, and, as a result, needed only *contemplate* what once demanded a total sacrifice, body and soul. As a result of writing, the unifying principle—the body as text—was lost, and a new organizing principle had to be found within the order of language itself.

The alternative, perhaps, was to find solace in the allegiance to a favorite god in a polytheistic universe. We find an example of such a transformation in the story of the conversion of Lucius in Apuleius's *Metamorphosis* (Nock 125) in which a young man led by love into careless dabbling in magic was changed into the shape of an ass. The story revolves around the eventual restoration of his human shape through the intervention of the goddess Isis, and of his subsequent devotion to the goddess in a series of ever-deepening spiritual transformations (Nock 125). But what seemed to be lacking was a religious center that could reunite individual and social aspirations, a center which reappeared, according to Frye, only with the concept of logos and a hieratic conception of language inherited by Stoicism and Christianity from Plato.

It is perhaps in this sense that we should understand A. D. Nock's argument that the concept of conversion cannot be primarily associated with pagan religions in classical antiquity. Unlike primitive religions, and certainly unlike Christianity, pagan religions of the classical period were not founded on an all-or-nothing proposition. The Greek and Egyptian religions did not demand body and soul of their adherents but were based on the regular observance of rites. It was enough to fulfill one's religious obligations during the appropriate holidays and then go on with one's life. The complex history of assimilation of various outside religious customs and gods in the Greek world testifies to the lack of organized exclusiveness of its religion, an exclusiveness which was fundamental to all the great proselytizing religions and a predominant feature in the Judaic tradition (Nock 1–32).

Although pagan religions and cults on the whole lacked the organized, totalizing assertiveness of the hieratic Judeo-Christian tradition, there were, as Nock points out, a number of religious and philosophical movements of antiquity in which the idea of conversion appeared, and which were instrumental in laying the groundwork for the Christian vision of the world. He maintains that the concept of conversion in religion emerged with the establishment of a permanent seat of religious authority at Delphi and with the birth of the Dionysiac and Orphic cults. The cult of Dionysus, not unlike Christianity, demanded total homage and submission from every man. Euripides's description of Dionysus disguised as a mortal speaking before the ruler Pentheus recalls to Nock "the Christian saint before a Roman magistrate" (25). The service of Dionysus meant "ecstasy and liberation and a curious sense of holiness which goes hand in hand with a fierce hatred of the man who 'fights against god' " (*Bacchae* 45, 325). In this context, Euripides also uses the phrase "kicks against the goads" (*Bacchae* 795), which eventually finds its way into the description of the conversion of Saul in Acts (Nock 25). But Nock insists that the idea of conversion and personal salvation truly emerged only with Orphism in the fifth century B.C. The Orphic life propounded an asceticism consisting of "abstinence from eating animal flesh and wearing woolen clothes, and contact with birth and death, respect for the holy writings, contempt for the body or soul's tomb, and a general preoccupation with expectations of a future life which the soul will enjoy thanks to discipline and initiation on earth" (Nock 26).

Both Orphism and the Dionysiac cult emerged in a period of social unrest, a time of "religious anxiety which showed itself in a desire for purification" (Nock 25). Indeed, as William James observes, conversion and salvation often have less to do with what we are turning toward than what we are turning away from: "Now with most of us the sense of our present wrongness is a far more distinct piece of our consciousness than is the imagination of any positive ideal that we can aim at. In a majority of cases, indeed, the sin almost exclusively engrosses the attention, so that conversion is a process of striving away from sin rather than of striving toward righteousness" (64). The motivational power of the conviction of sin was well understood by ancient writers. Horace, for example, tells of how, having neglected his duties to the gods, he was suddenly converted by a thunderclap out of a clear sky, a phenomenon for which he could find no scientific explanation (*Odes* 1.34.175).

Although Nock attributes the beginnings of the concept of conversion to the Orphic and Dionysiac cults, he concedes that the idea did not become firmly implanted in Western thinking until the rise of Greek philosophy. As in the cults, the idea that humankind needed to be rescued from a world in which things had gone drastically wrong was an important feature of the philosophical schools. As John Baillie comments in his *Baptism and Conversion*, "Most of these schools did call men to a new and radically different way of life, such as demanded a complete change of heart; a renunciation of the old man and an acceptance of a severe new discipline" (55). But unlike the pagan cults, philosophy presented its message in a unified and systematic way. The cults failed, Nock tells us, because they lacked an organized form of representation both in writing and in a living church. The philosophical schools, by contrast, not only maintained a permanent home for esoteric study but also produced an exoteric literature addressed to a general public. This new literary appeal offered "intelligible explanations of phenomena" and "promoted life with a scheme" (Nock 167), a discipline and a goal. Unlike the cults, the philosophical schools also had living teachers who were usually "canonized after death" (Nock 175). Plato, Nock indicates, "received cultus almost immediately after death and could soon be spoken of as Apollo's son" (175).

Equally as significant, Nock emphasizes the importance of Plato's prose style in the overall success of the philosophical school. "In this respect Plato above all put philosophy on the map: the supreme stylistic value of his writing gave them a public which they might otherwise have lacked" (179). As Northrop Frye has shown us, however, it was not only a superior literary style that attracted readers to Plato but the new forms of unified thought which Plato was able to produce in continuous prose. What emerged was a "revolution in language" based on a logical system of thought made possible by writing. Frye identifies this new hieratic use of language with the concept of logos:

> In the later Classical period Plato's sense of a superior order that only language, in both its verbal and mathematical forms, can approach merges with the conception generally identified as *logos.* This is a conception of a unity of consciousness or reason, suggested by the fact that properly-constructed verbal sequences seem to have inherent power of compelling assent. In Stoicism, and in Christianity in a different way from the beginning, the conception of *logos* acquires both a religious and politi-

> cal dimension: it is seen as a possible means of uniting human society both spiritually and temporally. (211)

The fact that the concept of conversion may have come to fruition first in the philosophical schools may seem somewhat surprising to many who have claimed the term for religion alone. But if we consider that conversion presupposes a unity of consciousness only possible with the advent of an integrated and systematic form of expression, the link between conversion and philosophy should cause no surprise at all. The hieratic form of writing makes ideology possible insofar as it produces a structured system of belief which "compels assent" and polarizes human behavior. And ideology was what distinguished Christianity from other religions of the time, a fact which was responsible, at least in part, for its success. We must bear in mind, however, that ideology in the philosophical schools and in Christianity did not only mean the key to membership in a privileged group. It was also, and perhaps more importantly, a personal possession designed to make people feel "at home in the universe" and at peace with themselves. Hieratic writing offered the possibility of uniting social and individual aspirations, enabling individuals to conceive of the self as a unified and distinct subject by internalizing the system of social valuations of the group to which they belonged and making this system part of their own identity.

It has often been noted that the philosophical schools exhibit profound parallels with Christianity. Socrates with his "sense of mission, quest for the basis of right conduct, and power for attracting and influencing disciples," not to mention his ultimate martyrdom, has often been compared with Christ (Nock 55). As Nock puts it, "Adhesion to Socrates meant giving your very soul to him" (55). Plato speaks of epistrophe, or the "turning around of the soul," as the very object of a philosophical education (Nock 179). But nowhere in the philosophical tradition are the parallels more evident than in the Stoic school. Scholars agree that Stoicism exercised a crucial influence on the apostle Paul, whose conversion on the road to Damascus, as the first recorded Christian conversion, became a prototype for those that followed. It was the Greco-Roman influence and particularly the Stoic concept of *Weltbürgertum* which provided the background in which Paul transformed the original nationalistic Judeo-Christian movement into a universalistic savior-god religion.

Paul's preaching and writing as well as New Testament accounts of his life and conversion presented an entirely new kind of eschatology to the pagan world. Reports of Paul's sermons and those of other Christians of that time describe how Christianity depicted life after death in the starkest of contrasts. To become a Christian meant the possibility of an eternity of heavenly bliss, while to remain pagan meant an eternity of torture and damnation. Christianity seemed to thrive on a polarity which inverted the ordinary conceptions of weakness and strength. The jailor petitions his prisoners, Silas and Paul, with the words, "What must I do to be saved?" Paul's conversion is itself a testimony to this radical dualism. Initially setting out to find and persecute followers of Christ, he suddenly reverses his inner orientation and becomes a Christian himself, later to be persecuted.

But if conversion is an important theme in Paul, the diverse accounts of his own conversion indicate that the depiction in writing of the inner life and its fundamental transformations was still a central problem. Paul himself tells us little about his conversion; from what he does say, however, he gives the impression that it was a private, internal experience. In Galatians 1, for example, he declares how God was pleased "to reveal his son in me." Howard Clark Kee stresses the significance of the expression "in me" (*en emoi*), since Paul could more easily have said "to me" (55). But Paul is unable to elaborate further on this experience of interiority. This relatively sparse autobiographical treatment of an experience which we have come to see as central to the Pauline doctrine is compensated for by the more familiar story of Paul's conversion in Acts. Here, as Kee indicates, Paul's abrupt change of heart is described in terms of an external confrontation which includes the sudden blinding and the hidden voice identified as Christ's which chastises Saul for his persecution of Christians (an activity which is likened to a self-destructive "kicking against the goads"). Kee, among others, contends that this description is a product of a literary imagination, "exploiting the literary traditions of the Greco-Roman world" for propagandist purposes (59). The gospel writer's familiarity with Euripides' metaphor of rebellion certainly reinforces the argument. Indeed, although we might understand this description of Paul's conversion on a purely metaphoric level, it does not seem to belong to a strictly hieroglyphic mode of expression, since its formulation also operates on a logical level—the image of blinding and the transition from a visual to a verbal message, as well as the literary metaphor of rebellion, all corresponding to a larger formula, a universal conception of conversion to be utilized as a personal model by others.

In contrast to this, there was another, more popular story of conversion attributed to Paul which seems to defy a hieratic understanding of language and approaches a more purely hieroglyphic conception. Speaking of the period in which he himself was converted near Damascus, Paul tells a group of nonbelievers in Ephesus of how he met a lion, spoke with it, converted it, and baptized it in a river (Macmullen 186). The lion, we are told, henceforth became celibate and took up the life of an ascetic. From our own point of view the story seems inscrutable unless interpreted in a purely metaphoric way. Yet Ramsay Macmullen argues that a pagan audience in Paul's time would have taken the story absolutely literally, seeing in it a demonstration of *virtus* in the speaker (186). But if we are guided by Frye's evolutionary conception of language use, we must recognize that the distinction is improperly framed and that the uneducated pagan would probably have understood Paul's story in neither way—or, more accurately, in both ways at once. This is to say that the either-or categories which we so naturally ascribe to language had not fully developed in the consciousness of the day. The pagan understood only the concrete meanings of the signs, thus hearing a message that literally fused the subjective and the objective world in a way which we can no longer comprehend, except perhaps in dreams.

There is general consensus that the depiction of the self as a psychological phenomenon originates with the Christian confession, most notably the *Confessions* of Augustine in the fourth century A.D. But as Michel Foucault illustrates in his study of the classical *hypomnēmata*, the shift to an interiorized idea of the self was a gradual phenomenon and did not represent a sudden departure from the classical tradition ("On the Genealogy of Ethics," 359–72). Already becoming popular in Plato's day, the hypomnemata was basically a notebook or copybook which contained observations of events and references to readings and conversations—in short, anything that might prove useful to writers in their daily activities. Nevertheless, Foucault takes care to qualify that this technical extension of the memory should not be confused with a confession or a personal diary. The point was not "to bring the *arcana conscientiae* to light," nor was it "to pursue the indescribable [or] . . . reveal the hidden, but, on the contrary, to collect the already said, to reassemble that which one could hear or read, and this to an end which is nothing less than the constitution of oneself" (365). According to Foucault, the classical ideal in the constitution and care of the self could generally be described as *self-mastery* (360). But from the time of Plato onward, the idea of self-mastery took an increasingly inward turn. In Plato's day it was considered a necessary corollary of power—the ability to rule over one's household and to carry out one's civic responsibilities. By the time of the late Stoics, however, the idea of self-mastery had become more austere and inwardly directed. One became a master of oneself because one was not a master of one's fate. The difference between the Stoic and the Christian conceptions of the self, Foucault argues, must therefore be understood not as an opposition between "tolerance and austerity" but rather as "two different forms of austerity," the former linked to an "aesthetics of existence," the latter linked to an incorporation of a transcendental model of social authority (366). This internalizing of authority necessitated a divided view of the self: a confessional self representing the natural consciousness or ego (which was susceptible to the influences of Satan) and an interlocuting self-as-other representing the supreme standards of a good God. Christian rebirth was therefore not so much a divestment of an old self as it was a denial and an imprisoning of that self and an identification with an other by accepting a new identity as one's own prison guard. Baptism may be traditionally interpreted as the ritual washing of the newborn soul, but the image of new converts submitting themselves completely to the ritual submergence also undeniably conjures up the image of drowning, of repression—a kind of ultimate test of faith in the Other.

CHAPTER 2

The Hieratic Phase

THE MOST FAMOUS early example of the Christian split-consciousness is Augustine's *Confessions.* From the very beginning of the *Confessions* we are aware of a narrating "I," or converted self, making itself subject to a form of authority projected as a silent, omnipotent interlocutor as it recollects the telos of its unconverted past. The result, as Eugene Vance points out, is a "dialectic between a converted self and a self-as-other," the consummation of which "would seem to come at the moment when the past and present are about to merge, when the I of the narrative past is about to join the I that is writing" (5). Vance argues, however, that to see the *Confessions* only in this way—as a conversion narrative which ends in the synthesis of the "I"—does not account for the last three books of the *Confessions,* in which Augustine questions the nature of time and human memory and interprets the book of Genesis.

According to Vance, Augustine's real conversion is at bottom a transformation in the use of language, a restructuring of identity through the discovery of the fallibility of certain forms of discourse and through the painful incorporation of new forms. It is no coincidence, Vance argues, that Augustine's acquisition of language and his conversion are both associated with images of mutilation and torture. Indeed, Augustine speaks of his formal language training at school in terms of corporal punishment: "Hence I was sent to school to acquire learning, the utility of which, wretched child that I was, I did not know. Yet if I was slow in learning, I was beaten. This method was praised by our forebears, many of whom had passed through this life before us and had laid out the hard paths we were to follow. Thus were both toil and sorrow multiplied for the sons of Adam" (26). As Augustine's narrative nears the period of conversion, we also note that the intensification of emotion ascribed to the unconverted "I" is depicted by images of a deformed and mutilated human body. Shortly before the conversion, God reveals Augustine to himself as if in a mirror: "You took me from behind my own back, which was where I had put myself during the time when I did not want to be observed by myself, and you set me in front of my own face so that I could see how foul a sight I was—crooked, filthy, spotted and ulcerous" (173). We may be reminded here of the mutilations of the body in primitive ceremonies of rebirth, but in this case the mutilation seems to describe not so much a writing on the human body as a recognition or a *reading* of sinful self's deformity by the almost-converted self in the presence of the divine Other.

The hidden cause of this mutilation is revealed only later in Augustine's discussion of Genesis, when God is described as the archetypal writer. Most significant, the metaphoric *tabula* upon which God writes his holy Word is skin:

> For heaven shall be folded up like a scroll, and now it is stretched over us like a skin. For your divine scripture is of all the more sublime authority because those mortals, through whom you gave it to us, have died their deaths. And you know Lord, you know how you clothed men with skins when their sin became mortal. And so you have like a skin stretched out the firmament of your book, that is, your words which so well agree together, and which through the agency of mortal men, you have placed above us. . . . I do not know, Lord, I do not know any writings so pure, so apt to persuade me to confess, to bow my neck to your yoke and to take service with you for nothing. (326)

This skin which God holds rolled up like the parchment of a completed scroll is the surface of the existent as it is unrolled in time, its differentiations over time composing the hieroglyphic language that God has inscribed on it. Human writings, or more precisely, the biblical scriptures, are for Augustine enunciations or performances of this divine script which are to be continually reread and reinterpreted in the light of the present. "For your divine Scripture is of all the more sublime authority because those mortals, through whom you gave it to us have died their deaths." According to Vance, Augustine's conception of original sin—human alienation from God—is precisely the "alienation into the signifying chain" by which individuals no longer accept themselves as a hieroglyph of God's divine scripture but presume to adopt a language of their own. Human salvation is possible only by a return to the primal state, with the reestablishment of the person as hieroglyph and God as archetypal writer.

> Stretched out beneath this "sky of skies" is the scroll of the firmament, a layer of "skin" where the primal dictation of creation is dispensed as a written text, a scripture. But this Scripture, like the Scripture at our disposal today, is impelled and sustained by force of the creative—and recreative—oral performance. Enunciation, then, is the mode of oral and prophetic truth, of auctoritas; the "writing" of the Scriptures is only ulterior meditation, merely a supplement. The skin of the scroll once covered man, who was a hieroglyph of authority. When Adam and Eve sinned, however, they covered the true text of the skin with the garments of an alien world. Martyrs, by contrast, are men who refuse to cover themselves with the skins of this world and with the fig leaves of false eloquence, and who continue to articulate God's authority to sinners in the "infirmity" below. (8–9)

Augustine's exegesis of Genesis is therefore an attempt to return metaphorically to the original state of humankind as text through hieratic writing. In order to make this transformation possible, Augustine must, in Vance's words, "scuttle the discourse of the self in favor of the discourse of the Other" (13). The confessional act thus necessarily becomes supplanted by the act of interpretation; the depiction of a conditional self on the road to salvation falls away in favor of a hermeneutical performance of God's divine writing, whose words "so well agree together."

Augustine's true conversion is therefore not a unification of a divided "I" but a transcendence of the idea of the self-as-referent and the dissolution of that deictic self into the authorizing power of the Other. What Augustine has accomplished is to reach the conceivable limits in hieratic writing, where language and life form a strict totality. But as Vance points out, language for Augustine is not "about life." Indeed, it is precisely the reverse: "life is about language" (17). Within the hieratic order of language founded on a single text—the Bible—life acquires its coherence and meaning. Unlike the hypomnemata, which merely brought together the fragmentary logos in the spatial setting of a notebook, the confession, as conceived by Augustine, set forth a formula whereby personal and universal history could be integrated into a strict figural unity in which not only the present and past but also the future was already contained (13). This kind of totality is the end and culmination of hieratic thinking; nothing more could be accomplished except by way of fulfilling and perfecting this pyramidic order in the social realm, by transforming it into a political reality.

There is no more fitting political manifestation of the transcendental hieratic order than the Catholic church. Its emphasis on a hierarchical totality determines not only its basic organization but also its various means of achieving conformity—the most important being the practice of *exomologēsis*, or oral confession. As practiced in the church, oral confession, whether public or private, has an overriding jurisdictional purpose (Snoeck 22–31). This function is perhaps most evident in the very early church, where absolution and the restoration of the individual into the community were contingent upon extremely severe forms of penance (Snoeck 8). Gradually, probably because of the growing influence of secular authority over private life, the overtly jurisdictional aspect of the confessional became less obvious. But it is perhaps for the same reason that, as Foucault points out, the Catholic church sought an ever more subtle, psychological control over the individual by demanding an increasingly detailed and internalized examination of conscience.

Conversion too became more and more rigidly defined by the church. By the Renaissance, both the confessional and the idea of conversion had become so firmly entrenched in church doctrine that, as Jacob Burckhardt tells us, many of the "more powerful natures" began to resist staunchly the church's attempt to control their moral natures (514). What was difficult for certain exceptional individuals to accept in this doctrine of salvation was the fact that a liberating act had become caught up in ecclesiastical concerns. The need for liberation from dogma and ecclesiastical control manifested itself in what Burckhardt calls a sixteenth-century "contempt for repentance" (514). Cardan declares, "I repent at nothing; else I should be of all men the most miserable" (Non poenitere ullius rei quam voluntarie effécerim, etiam quae male cessisset.) (*De vita propria*, chap. 13; quoted in Burckhardt 514). Machiavelli ventures even further when he proclaims his disgust for the church's eschatological means of control, calling it a menace to the state and to public freedom (*Discourses* 278–79). The resistance to the church through the written word indicates a return to writing as a creative rather than a performative act. Writing becomes an assertion of inner authority which is no longer dependent on the hermeneutical performance of a "divinely" inspired text.

Montaigne's essay "Of Repentance" addresses precisely this issue of inner and outer authority. The very term "repentance," which emphasizes control over liberation, is unacceptable to the writer, who asserts, "I rarely repent" (179). Montaigne thus prepares the way for a more internalized and liberated approach to salvation: "There is no one who, if he listens to himself, does not discover in himself a pattern all his own, a ruling pattern, which struggles against education and against the tempest of the passions that oppose it" (186). Montaigne's justification comes from the self illuminated by the light of reason: "God must touch our hearts. Our conscience must reform by itself through the strengthening of our reason" (194). This self-justification opposes traditional concepts of rebirth and renewal as an experience brought about by outside forces. But Montaigne is careful not to offend ecclesiastical authority and uses a classical illustration to make his point: "I do not follow the belief of the sect of Pythagoras, that men take on a new soul when they approach the images of the Gods to receive their oracles" (188).

For the Renaissance mind, subjectivity came to be associated with the Cartesian cogito. The belief that being itself was grounded in consciousness and that even the existence of God could be deduced from this premise gave reasonable individuals the courage to examine their own lives and to stand up to the authority of churchmen and princes. It allowed them to challenge the veracity of traditional dogmas and beliefs. Although Montaigne's concept of an internal truth was still partly founded on a hieratic form of thinking which substitutes reason and logic for a divine logos, it constituted a liberation both from the reliance on a single textual source and from the servitude to an organization claiming the sole right to interpret that source. But Montaigne's form of rational subjectivity also approached a demotic way of thinking, since authority was now seen as residing in the individual. As a result, each experience had to be judged in its own right; truth had to correspond to the situation instead of the situation to the truth. By shifting the burden of judgment from an external authority to an internal process of verification, the individual acquired a completely new outlook on the problem of personal salvation. People were now responsible for their own soul. Their personal well-being depended on their own judgment and ability. More important, this new salvation of the self depended on a new form of writing—the essay—through which the "ruling pattern" of the self could be "tried," discovered, and elucidated.

In eighteenth-century France, secular writing became much more openly hostile to ecclesiastical rigidity, particularly in the area of ethics and morality. Sex became an especially potent weapon by which people could flaunt their rebellion against the strict moral injunctions of the church. But, as Foucault points out, the church may have played a role of complicity in fostering this awakened eighteenth-century interest in sex, not so much only because of its repressive attitude toward sexuality, but because of its increasing emphasis on "inciting sexual discourse" in the confessional. By the eighteenth century the confessor enjoined the penitent to "tell everything, . . . not only consummated acts, but also sensual touchings, all impure gazes, all obscene remarks . . . all consenting thoughts" ("The Repressive Hypothesis" 304). As Foucault observes, this pastoral injunction to "confess everything" also finds many secular equivalents in the eighteenth century—even in the confessional attitudes of such extremists as the Marquis de Sade. Sade's advice to other writers in his *One Hundred Twenty Days of Sodom*, Foucault tells us, could have been found in any eighteenth-century confessional manual. "Your narrations must be decorated with the most numerous and searching details; the precise way and the extent to which we may judge how the passion you describe relates to human manners and man's character is determined by your willingness to disguise no circumstance; and what is more, the least circumstance is apt to have an immense influence upon the procuring of that kind of sensory irritation we expect from your stories" (*One Hundred and Twenty Days* 271). Although the goals of the Catholic confession and the Sadean form of self-exposé are very different, on a purely emotive level they do have a peculiar similarity of purpose, both entailing a certain liberation, a quality of making oneself into a subject for the purpose of securing release. But the Catholic confession (apart from the emotional excitement engendered by the act of confession itself) is dependent on the final authoritative pronouncement of absolution by the priest. The Sadean liberation, by contrast—"that kind of sensory irritation"—is both dependent on the risk it poses for itself in the face of moral authority and on the conviction that the moral authority of the church cannot prevail against the powers of nature.

This belief in the ultimate power of nature over any form of ecclesiastical authority is perhaps most evident in Sade's anticonversion story, "Dialogue between a Priest and a Dying Man." The story is one of Sade's earliest dated literary works as well as one of the earliest modern statements of open atheism. Written in prison after his wife's family had succeeded in permanently incarcerating him for his sexual excesses, the "Dialogue" tells the story of a priest who comes to convert a dying sinner, to obtain his repentance and to give him absolution. The dying man turns out to be a reluctant convert, however. Point by rational point, the invalid wins over the priest to his own amoral and hedonistic way of thinking. In the end, it is the priest who becomes converted to the pleasures of the flesh, joining the dying man in one last orgy in the arms of six beautiful women. The story is of particular interest from a philosophical point of view because it combines open atheism with open amoralism. Not only is Sade denying the divine creation of the universe, but he rejects the ethical character of nature: "Since she has equal need of vices and of virtues, when it has pleased Nature to impel me to the former, she has done so, and when she has decided on the latter, she has inspired in me desires for them, and I have yielded to them in the same way. Look only to her laws for the sole cause of our human inconsistency; and don't look to her laws for any principles other than her own wishes and needs" (16).

The "Dialogue" thus represents a watershed in the history of rational subjectivism. Sade doesn't merely wrest the idea of an absolute morality out of the hands of a Supreme Being, he refuses to reinstate a comforting version of it in the name of secular reason. There is no moral pattern for one to discern in nature, particularly in one's own nature. Words must therefore be used in a way that corresponds to the things they describe. Sadean rationalism is completely and uncompromisingly demotic: life no longer reflects language; language must reflect life. Human beings are suddenly set adrift. They are free to follow the caprices of their own nature. They have no one other than themselves to turn to for guidance. They must conclude, as the early Sartre did, that they are condemned to be free.

The image of the deathbed conversion is not new in literature and can probably be found anywhere there is a clash of extremes. In the case of the "Dialogue," it not only parodies the traditional Christian deathbed conversion but also echoes a deathbed conversion literature that arose out of the Stoic school, of which Sade may well have been aware. Indeed, in her well-known essay on Sade, Simone de Beauvoir argues that Sade is ironically a Stoic at heart (54–55). His exploits were typically a kind of self-flagellation through the mortification of others, an annihilation of Nature's meaninglessness by insensitizing himself to its caprices through excess. At the edge of the abyss, completely unable to find a true point of communication with others, Sade must have sensed the desperate loneliness of his freedom. The alternative to this alienation was to abuse others physically, partly out of revenge, partly because by dominating their bodies he was incorporating their lives into his own. It is no coincidence that after he was imprisoned and deprived of this physical contact, he became an insatiable glutton. His only way to belong to an alien and meaningless world was to ingest it, to make it his alone.

We might also conjecture that for the imprisoned Sade, writing comes to take the place of physical mutilation of others. Indeed, one of the sexual perversions for which Sade was first taken to court seems to be particularly indicative of this need to inscribe one's authoritative presence on others. According to the deposition of Rose Kailair in 1768, Sade "made various incisions [on her body] with a small knife or penknife, [and] poured red wax and white wax in greater quantity on these wounds." Equally as startling is Sade's claim to absolute authority during this cruel episode. When Kailair begged Sade not to let her die before taking Easter Communion, Sade told her that he would "confess her himself" (*The Marquis de Sade* 1953 ed. 214). It is precisely this combination of desires—the need to become a mutilating god—which also seems to inspire Sade's writings. In the Sadean fictional universe, the author takes upon himself the role of the authoritarian Other, inscribing his inner urges on an imaginary world of human bodies, forcing a procession of characters to undergo rituals of torture and mutilation in order to become members of his fiercely totalizing fantasy. For Sade, writing is not a ritual performance of a transcendental order, nor is it a rational means to self-discovery; it is a mechanism by which social authority can be metaphorically defaced and annihilated. Its ultimate aim, as in the "Dialogue," is the "unconversion" of the converter, the reinitiation of the priest into the power and mystery of his own body.

If Sade's unhappy fate underscores the hopelessness of achieving such an uncompromising self-justification in the real world, his success as a writer reflects the change in the nature of authority in the eighteenth century that made self-justification possible in writing. The very idea of writing as a form of violence against the social order seems impossible without some kind of complicity, a complicity which in eighteenth-century France could be established only through the back door of sex. We might be surprised to learn that of all the writing that emerged from Sade's Vincennes prison/château (and the Bastille) between 1778 and 1790, most of it explicitly pornographic, the "Dialogue" was one of the only works that Sade himself suppressed. Compared with most of his other work, its atheistic message now seems mild indeed. And yet, as the American editor of Sade's collected works points out, in a world where even such freethinkers as Diderot and d'Alembert were careful to avoid open disagreement with the church, a statement of atheism and the amorality of nature constituted a much graver offense than "mere" pornography (*The Marquis de Sade* 1965 ed. 164). The following statement on atheism in the *Encyclopedie* was one of the few signed by both Diderot and d'Alembert: "Even the more tolerant of men will not deny that the judge has the right to repress those who profess atheism, and even to condemn them to death if there is no other way of freeing society from them. . . . If he can punish those who harm a single person, he doubtless has as much right to punish those who wrong an entire society by denying that there is a God. Such a man may be considered as an enemy of all men" (*The Marquis de Sade* 164).

It really was a question of authority at stake. If the truth about the world was within reach of each individual, and the recognition of that truth was a corroboration, an inductive response within the mind of each reader, then autobiography acquired unprecedented authority and power. It became a secret theater par excellence for self-display—first for the writing consciousness reading itself, but ultimately for the reading consciousness interpreting and reenacting on the stage of its own fantasy the manifest script of the Other. It was this new complicity between authors and readers that established a new form of authority to rival the old and that set the necessary preconditions for modern autobiography.

CHAPTER 3

The Demotic Phase

ROUSSEAU'S *Confessions*, perhaps more than any earlier autobiography, marked the beginning of the "historically" conditioned modern autobiography. Some critics will go as far as to say that in the proper sense of the word, autobiography really begins with *The Confessions*. The fact that a new word was coined near the turn of the nineteenth century to describe a genre already laden with terminology ("hypomnemata," "commentarii," "vita," "confession," "memoir," "apologia") is in itself significant in that it reflects an awareness of the inadequacy of old terms to convey new, more radically self-assertive aims. The term "autobiography" distinguished itself from the other words in that it rendered visible for the first time the reflexive component of the self—"autos." This self, which now came first, was the interpreter of its own life ("bios"), through the directed activity of writing ("graphos"). For Rousseau, the past—or at least his memory of the past—becomes the field in which meaning is discerned and assigned to the present. The difference between the word "confession" as Rousseau understood it and a religious confession like that of Augustine and his successors is therefore profound. For Rousseau, a person is a product of the sum of his or her experiences. Experience has corrupted one's essential nature, turning people into the unhappy beings they have become. Augustine, by contrast, asserts that experience does not contribute to inner development. One experience is as good as another; a person grows in spite of his or her experience because of God's secret guidance and grace. Rousseau's appeal to authority is demotic; Augustine's, hieratic. This difference is more understandable if we look at the point of view taken by each writer. Augustine submits to God's authority and grace, entreating the reader to do the same. Rousseau, by contrast, continually petitions his readers for their favorable judgment, sometimes appealing to their reasonableness, their empathy, even their forbearance. Rousseau's description of himself on the final day of judgment makes his position in relation to temporal and spiritual authority abundantly clear. The author presents himself as standing before the supreme Author and Judge with his book in hand (and the assenting readership it implies in mind), firmly expecting these proofs to mollify God's verdict. Compared with Augustine's reverence for the great wisdom and power of God, Rousseau's persistent belief in a "pact" between writer and reader has made God into a rather democratic judge.

Rousseau's insistence on self-justification before his fellow human beings demonstrates the new cultural function of modern autobiography. Earlier religious confessions were essentially didactic, based on a tripartite formula of self-condemnation, redemption through Christ, and praise of a new life in God. Rousseau's *Confessions*, in contrast, emphasizes precisely the opposite intentions: praise of the unspoiled soul of the child before its corruption by culture, self-justification through an appeal to this state of primal innocence, and lamentation for his inescapably unhappy situation in society. In this sense, Rousseau's boast at the beginning of his book that he has "entered upon a performance which is without precedent" is true. Even secular memoirs and autobiographies before *The Confessions*, like their religious counterparts, were exemplary narratives written by extraordinary men. Autobiographers such as Vico saw no need for self-justification, since society already approved and encouraged their efforts to write their life stories (Fisch 1–7). For Rousseau, however, the onus for justification falls entirely on the individual. Without the reader's complicity and understanding, the author's appraisal of himself has little or no value.

What distinguishes Rousseau's work as well as many subsequent modern autobiographies from the autobiography as exemplum is that history is used not merely as an instructional tool but as a medium through which the writer assigns meaning and purpose to his or her life. This new role for autobiography—individuals exploring their memory through writing in order to discover in it a significant pattern by which they can interpret their present life and orient themselves toward the future—lends itself especially to the adaptation of the Christian notion of conversion. For Rousseau, this "conversion" takes place on an October afternoon in 1749 on the road to Vincennes. Echoing the conversion story of St. Paul, Rousseau's experience ends with a confirmation of his vocation as a writer. Like Paul, Rousseau enters the city of his destination and receives counsel as to his future role. In this case, however, the mentor is not a persecuted Christian but a persecuted, secular philosophe—Diderot. It is Diderot who convinces Rousseau that he should enter the Dijon writing contest, which he is destined to win. The subject of Rousseau's essay, significantly, reflects precisely the inversion of values, the attack against the established order that we find in Sade: to the question as to whether the arts and sciences have improved human morals, Rousseau responds with a resounding no.

Only through writing about the self is Rousseau able to recollect his history of failure and to read in (or into) it the pattern of his present unhappy condition. But equally as important, only through writing can Rousseau convince his readership of his own "truth." This is the ultimate form of conversion, the mass conversion of a reading public by an individual. Autobiography in this modern sense creates a verbal facsimile of a world in which the author's symbolic presence overrules cultural forms of authority already implicit in language. What we find in Rousseau strikes a point somewhere short of Sade's uncompromising extremism. *The Confessions* remains within the bounds of possibility because we recognize in his motives for action traces of our own motives and because his acts themselves remind us of our own uncommitted ones.

The difference between Sade and Rousseau on this point is only a matter of degree. Both are trying to convert the reader to an extremely subjective worldview; both are trying to gain the reader's complicity in indicting society for its role as a perverter and falsifier of the true and worthy natural self. If we hesitate to connect the blunt, sexual aggression of Sade with the subtler, more complex and timid relationships of Rousseau, we have only to think of Rousseau's exhibitionism during his adolescence:

> I haunted dark alleys and lonely spots where I could expose myself to women from afar off in the condition in which I should have liked to be in their company. What they saw was nothing obscene, I was far from thinking of that: it was ridiculous. The absurd pleasure I got from displaying myself before their eyes is quite indescribable. There was only one step for me still to make to achieve the experience I desired, and I have no doubt that some bold girl would have afforded me the amusement, as she passed, if I had possessed the courage to wait. (91)

But unlike Sade, Rousseau does not achieve the sexual union he so much desires. Instead he is chased and caught by "a big man with a big moustache and a big sword," an image replete with its connotations of castration. Throughout *The Confessions* Rousseau alludes to his difficulties in achieving sexual control, but he is too timid to transform his urges into actions. His desires must be achieved by means other than direct ones.

To continue in a Freudian vein: writing supplies for Rousseau the needed substitute phallus. One might say, with a slight alteration of Bulwer-Lytton's famous maxim, that Rousseau's transformation exemplifies the dictum, "The [pen is] mightier than the sword." Rather than becoming lost in psychotic repetition like Sade, Rousseau's original urge to expose himself is transformed into a highly sophisticated form of verbal self-display. By deliciously parading before us detailed accounts of his foibles and sins such as the one quoted above, he achieves the twofold effect which he could not achieve in adolescence, the mixture of affront and self-abasement, of sadism and masochism, that shocks and arouses our sympathies at the same time.

Rousseau's solution in *The Confessions* to create a verbal world in which a reconstructed self poses as a real self also calls to mind the pitiable gluttony of Sade. Rousseau has symbolically ingested an alienated culture to save himself from it. But in order to achieve this kind of salvation, he not only has literally had to imprison himself on the Isle de St. Pierre, he has also imprisoned a self in a book. James Olney alludes to this tendency in autobiography to immobilize the free-flowing quality of life. Expanding upon a quotation from Yeats—"It is possible that being is only possessed completely by the dead"—he reasons that being is possessed only when it becomes identical with meaning, and that meaning in turn is possible only after it has been taken out of the confused course of real life and transplanted in the symbolic world (*Metaphors of Self* 226). Thus by entombing the real self in the act of symbolizing it, the autobiographer creates the possibility of a resurrection, where meaning is again transformed into being in the very act of its consumption. Reading autobiography, in this sense, replicates metaphorically (as does Christianity) those primitive practices of cannibalism in which the body of the deceased was consumed in order to incorporate the special attributes of the individual. Reading the self thus offers the writer a kind of secularized "eternal life." Paul's admonition "the letter killeth," however true in an essentially nonliterate world, must, in a world where identity is dependent on the written word, undergo a rebirth; as Lacan inquires, "We should like to know how the spirit could live without the letter" (*Ecrits* 158)?

If modern autobiography offers writers the opportunity to save themselves by means of a symbolic transference, it remains to be seen just what this transference achieves. Certainly it does not mean a literal reconciliation between the subject and object. At best the world can be internalized, as Charles Altieri says, in a "dialogue of the subject with itself" (140). Nevertheless, Altieri argues, even this limited dialogue carries with it the possibility for salvation, for in recreating an image of the self in a book and offering it to others, one can hope to achieve the "absolute rhythms of experience":

> These rhythms are as much of the absolute as limited man can grasp, but by recognizing, for example, how development is an essentially lawful process of suffering and reconciliation, of loss and compensatory gains, one comes to trust in the recurrences informing life and to be content with what signs of the absolute he can discover. The result is not alienation but grace, the sense that man in his limited state has what may suffice for secular salvation. And the ultimate testimony of that salvation (as it was for Augustine in a different context) is that man can both satisfactorily compose his autobiography and offer it for the enrichment of others. (140)

In the case of Rousseau's *Confessions*, however, as in other modern autobiographies, it is clear that something more than the "enrichment of others" is at stake. Stephen Spender reminds us that confession always implies some sort of confessor figure who in the end absolves the individual on the condition that he carry out a prescribed penance. The need for absolution also seems to be an important feature of modern secular autobiography, but the question remains, Who is there to perform this rite? According to Spender, Rousseau addresses "the spirit of democracy" (121). He wants to be absolved of his sins in the eyes of a world which he brings down to his moral level, and yet, unlike the sincere Christian penitent, he wants to remain unchanged. Spender argues that there is "a lie concealed in his very method," because to justify oneself by degrading the reader is dishonest (121). It implies that since the writer is no good and no one can be better, there is no reason to make moral judgments. For this reason, Spender affirms, Rousseau "has always aroused suspicion" among readers (121).

But we must ask ourselves whether forgiveness is really the most important component in the confessional urge. At least we must try to determine what absolution means for the modern autobiographer. Is it perhaps enough to have confessed, regardless of the consequences, since, in the last resort, confession can be its own form of grace through self-punishment? Writers, taking upon themselves the mask of eiron, render themselves invulnerable through self-display. At the end of Rousseau's reading of his confessions, we find the audience silent—only Madame d'Egmont trembles visibly, then she too becomes silent. Perhaps it is this silence that the confessor needs most; that is, he needs to silence his judges, to deprive them of their judgments by his overwhelming display of self-disclosure.

Contrary to Spender's belief, even the basest confession is apt to find a sympathetic readership. This need not be so much a debasement of the reader as a recognition at some level of the inner correspondences between individuals. We need not have acted like Rousseau in order to identify with him. Moreover, as Janet Varner Gunn argues, if the reader constitutes a "position" in the text, then, as readers, we participate in this position in ways that open up new possibilities for being. In this sense, reading autobiography offers us the opportunity to participate in a form of ontological play; we live in and through the signifying materiality as if it were our own. Nevertheless, although we enter into this "as if" position seemingly of our own accord, in actuality it is the text that lures us to it and holds us there.

Although Rousseau's power over his audience depends on the authority of a historical consciousness, it also relies on a vital carryover from the Christian tradition, the belief in the essential unity of the human subject. This residual influence of a discursive tradition gives autobiographical writing its powerful new legitimacy. By reducing the transcendental subject to the status of a material product of historical cause and effect, Rousseau projects a form of writing (and reading) consciousness that takes the place of a transcendental presence. But unlike the Christian mode of transcendence, in which a divine authority necessarily precedes and determines the individual life, Rousseau's authority issues directly from the conventions of the autobiographical narrative, producing what Louis A. Renza calls a metafather fiction. "Psychologically fatherless and ideologically (if not in his literal discourse) godless, Rousseau the autobiographer evokes through his autobiographical act the chaos of absence, . . . He brings up his own discontinuous, arbitrary origins—his pastness which he tries to convert into being the fatherlike source of himself" (289–90).

Rousseau appropriates the Christian rebirth narrative in order to convert the reading public to a highly idiosyncratic point of view. Conversion at this level involves interpreting cultural inscriptions on the body (the natural self) as marks of repression; one performs the ritual of self-mutilation in order to project a liberated and enlightened imaginary social body with which both reader and writer can identify. From this imaginary perspective the reader perceives the essential interaction between self and world as a rational, lawful process that justifies its final result. Although "democratic" in its appeal, however, the underlying purpose of this form of self writing is to transform one's own authorial voice into the voice of the authorizing father, not only to save oneself from the authority of others but ultimately to inflict one's authority on them as well.

CHAPTER 4

Conversion and the Symbolic Order

FREUD'S *Interpretation of Dreams* consummates a century-long preoccupation with dreams and visions which began with the Romantics. Often only suppressed or disguised by the preceding neoclassical writers, this Romantic interest in the dream grew out of a dissatisfaction with the limitations of a purely rationalist, demotic conception of self. More often than not, nineteenth-century autobiographers with literary ability were less interested in showing the external circumstances of life—the grand gestures, monumental achievements, and public images—than with revealing the "inner self," its private feelings, motives, and desires. How could one represent in writing these "internal" preoccupations without tampering with empirical evidence, investing it with ulterior metaphoric significance, or rearranging the sequence of events? The dream provided a means by which an affective reality could be represented through modes of association that rivaled a straightforward "historical" account. The problem remained of how the writer was to integrate these new elements in autobiography without undermining the rational and empirical nature of the project. How was one to mediate between different, not necessarily compatible, forms of temporality? In short, although the dream may have provided a means for a more complex form of self-expression, it did not in itself legitimize that expression.

What was needed was a complete revision of the concept of the self, a rejection of the eighteenth-century rational model in favor of a more dynamic model of subjectivity. This the English Romantics found in German idealism—in particular, in Kant's paradigm of subjectivity—the so-called transcendental unity of apperception. If the dream provided new possibilities for representing an affective self-consciousness, Kantian theory offered the formal principles of order by which new, more complex modes of association could be integrated with a rationalist version of temporality. Nevertheless, the integration of a Kantian model of subjectivity into the literature of the self was a gradual process. Since modern autobiography was founded on rational presuppositions, an a priori conception of knowledge threatened to undermine the very discourse it was intended to supplement. Kant's notion of the subject as a formal activity rather than a substantive identity further problematized the fundamental nature of the autobiographical project. The full implications of Kantian idealism could be worked out only through a compromise between idealist and rationalist conceptions as in the Freudian metapsychology or by fictionalizing the notion of a de facto self-as-object—or by abandoning the concept of the subject altogether.

The rationalist dilemma of legitimizing an affective self-consciousness was complicated by a further problem. The notion of a permanent unity of identity had already been challenged by David Hume, who argued that a unifying center of consciousness is impossible to verify either logically or descriptively. Nietzsche went so far as to pronounce the notion of a unified, de facto subject an illusion, the product of conventions in writing. Indeed, as Paul Jay has argued, the idea of a unified self began to be undermined almost immediately after its institution as a genre of writing. A nineteenth-century autobiographical turn toward dreams and fantasy might well be understood as an attempt to reauthorize an inherited Christian notion of subjectivity which could not be supported by the new modes of rationalist consciousness.

One of the more striking nineteenth-century attempts to "reauthorize" the self is Thomas De Quincey's *Confessions of an Opium Eater* (1822). In these confessions, which De Quincey wrote at the age of thirty-five but which he revised and augmented until the end of his life, we are able to trace a progression of very different appeals to authority and to the gradual rejection of the conversion narrative as a legitimizing framework. William C. Spengemann's discussion of the evolution of autobiography as a literary form identifies De Quincey's work as a turning point in self-writing because of its change in attitude toward the authority of history (93). Like Augustine's *Confessions,* Spengemann argues, *Confessions of an Opium Eater* has a tripartite structure. This structure can be described quite simply as determined by the relation of the narrating self to the acting self in the text—in short, to the three temporal dimensions assigned to existence: past, present, and future. De Quincey's original *Confessions of an Opium Eater* is written from the point of view of a reformed addict, a stance analogous to the first nine books in Augustine's *Confessions*, where the reformed or converted self looks back on the unconverted sinner. But where Augustine's authority relies on a belief in an eternal truth situated outside of time, De Quincey's authority relies on the shared opinion of the readers that there is an objective approach to the past (historicity) and that health rather than sickness (addiction) is a necessary condition to achieve this historical point of view. It is inevitable, however, that autobiographers using a "historical approach" will inevitably reach a point, often identified by the "conversion experience," where they become one with the character and enter into a discourse of the present. Such narrators of the present have the option to continue their autobiography in diary form or else to choose another method of discourse.

Spengemann quite rightly argues that the most suitable discourse for the depiction of the self grounded in the present is the philosophical (98). In Augustine, the historical becomes the philosophical as soon as the narrator ceases to reflect upon images of his past selves and begins his speculations on the nature of being and time. Correspondingly, De Quincey gives up trying to fight the attraction of opium from the pose of a reformed or "converted" addict and launches into his present situation in the appendix to his *Confessions*, an addict once again. At this point, Spengemann states, De Quincey's real conversion takes place, when he takes up from the observation made at the end of the *Confessions* that "not the opium eater" but the opium, the thing renounced, "is the true hero of the tale, and the legitimate center on which the interest revolves" (100). Spengemann goes on to describe how both Augustine and De Quincey discover the limitations of this philosophical inquiry into the present and enter a third phase which he calls poetic autobiography. Augustine's transition takes place in the last books of the *Confessions*, when he adopts the "discourse of the Other" through hermeneutical interpretation of the book of Genesis. It is faith which leads Augustine on his pilgrimage through the past and present to a celebration of things to come within the divine order. For De Quincey, by contrast, the notion of the other has been inverted. Suffering due to an interminable addiction leads not to God and salvation but to the shadowy regions of the human psyche. For De Quincey, suffering is the "primary formation of the human system" (154–55). It is evidence, as Spengemann adds, of a world out of range of ordinary human consciousness, and for De Quincey, proof of an inner world made accessible only through dreams and images of earliest childhood which form the "hieroglyphic meaning of human suffering" (44).

Here De Quincey's speculations on dreaming not only reiterate the metaphor of a reading of authorizing inscriptions on the imaginary body, they also closely anticipate the Freudian discovery, both in its particulars (e.g. that dreams are linked to memories of earliest childhood) and in its central premise—"a dream is the representation of a wish." For what are wishes but the expression of desires that have not been, perhaps cannot be, actualized? Are not wishes, in short, the obverse side of repressions that form the very root of human suffering? These repressions, in De Quincey's view, derive from what he calls a "too intense life of the social instincts" (114), which we can associate with Freud's ego instincts, whose continual struggle to uphold a standard that reflects social limitations impedes and restructures the internal pathways of desire. Likely for this reason, De Quincey, like Freud, tends to think of dreaming as a secret language, associating it with the reading of coded inscriptions, particularly Egyptian hieroglyphics. For De Quincey, the mind itself was a palimpsest upon which the divine inscriptions were written:

> I am convinced . . . that the dread book of account, which the Scriptures speak of, is in fact the mind itself of each individual. Of this, at least, I feel assured, that there is no such thing as *forgetting* possible to the mind; a thousand accidents may, and will interpose a veil between our present consciousness and the secret inscriptions of the mind; accidents of the same sort will also rend away the veil; but alike, whether veiled or unveiled, the inscription remains forever; just as the stars seem to withdraw before the common light of day, whereas, in fact, we all know that it is the light which is drawn over them as a veil—and that they are waiting to be revealed, when the obscuring daylight shall have withdrawn. (104)

Through dreaming, De Quincey insists, we are able to return to these "secret inscriptions" of this "dread book of account" in the "palimpsest of the human brain." According to De Quincey, "The machinery for dreaming planted in the human brain was not planted for nothing. That faculty, in alliance with the mystery of darkness, is the one great tube through which man communicates with the shadowy. And the dreaming organ, in connection with the heart, the eye, and the ear, compose the magnificent apparatus which forces the infinite into the chambers of the human brain and throws dark reflections from eternities below all life upon the mirrors of the sleeping mind" (114). Only dreams can unify De Quincey's shattered life, bringing together "the nearer and more distant stages of life," representing the past "not as a succession but as parts of a coexistence" (40). Here, the rudimentary *Nacheinander* of rationalist consciousness gives way to the more mysterious *Nebeneinander* of human memory and the internal structuring powers of the mind in a way that remarkably foreshadows the age of psychoanalysis. De Quincey takes up the dreaming faculty as a new model of authority, heralding a new era of what Spengemann calls poetic autobiography. Thus, according to Spengemann, this new form of autobiography, which describes subsequent novels like Carlyle's *Sartor Resartus*, Dickens's *David Copperfield*, and Hawthorne's *Scarlet Letter*, "abandons all reference to the biographical event . . . to discover through a fictive action some ground upon which conflicting aspects of the writer's own nature might be reconciled in complete being" (132).

Spengemann's account of the development of De Quincey's confessions is accurate as far as it goes. But by setting Augustine and De Quincey under the same heading "poetic autobiography," he does not make necessary distinctions between hieratic and rationalist modes of consciousness. If Augustine's unity of subjectivity is based on the adoption of a transcendental authority anterior to being, De Quincey's subject is founded on the conviction about the a priori powers of the psyche, affirming a psychological rather than a Christian "discourse of the Other." This new transcendental relation is certainly reflected in De Quincey's initial enthusiasm about Kantian philosophy, which gave him a sense of "the profoundest revelation." Indeed, one of De Quincey's many unacted-upon resolutions was to retire to "the woods of Lower Canada," where he proposed to build "a cottage and a considerable library" in order to devote his life to the study and development of transcendentalism (Lindop 131–32).

Perhaps a greater tribute to the power of Kantian philosophy, however, was its devastating impact on De Quincey, of which the instability of his own life with its interminable addiction became the correlative and, perhaps even to some degree, the effect. "Let a man meditate but a little on this [theory of apperception] and other aspects of this transcendental philosophy, and he will find the steadfast earth itself rocking as it were beneath his feet" (*Collected Writings* 2:101). Just this lack of solidity is represented throughout the *Confessions*, especially in the last books, in which De Quincey seems to have abandoned any vestige of rationalist commentary and thrown his readers without recourse into the labyrinthine meanderings of his dreams. De Quincey remains convinced that dreaming opens the doors to a deeper self-knowledge, but he lacks the key by which to unlock the mysteries of his dreams. As a result, one dream image follows hard upon the other without any clear indication just what they are meant to signify. He may have found himself in what he called the cul-de-sac of Kantian subjectivity, but it was a position from which he could not retreat.

The breakdown of a "historical consciousness" is further exemplified by Carlyle's *Sartor Resartus*. Here the tension between a rationalist's historicizing view of the world and a subjectively conditioned metaphysical view becomes evident in the division of roles between the foreign protagonist Teufelsdröckh and his anonymous domestic editor. In *Sartor*, the authorial "I" seems unable to situate itself and alternates between the position of the editor and that of the protagonist. We know that the editor serves as a go-between, making the Kantian idealism of the German professor acceptable to the English public. We also know that Carlyle is decidedly in favor of the transcendentalism of Teufelsdröckh. But we come to this realization only after sifting through layers of self-protective irony. Carlyle's is an irony of uncertainty. The mock-seriousness of his inflated Germanic prose style disguises a fundamental Calvinist seriousness which can no longer be openly displayed.

As Paul Jay points out, "*Sartor Resartus* reflects that condition of irony that nineteenth-century historiography fell into when the historian discovered how aesthetic and fictional his facticity and objectivity were" (109). This discovery is yet another reason for the split roles of editor and protagonist. By making this division, Carlyle separates rationalist historical consciousness from the autobiographical situation itself. Teufelsdröckh, in response to questions about his biography, sends the editor six paper bags filled with "miscellaneous masses of Sheets, and oftener Shreds and Snips . . . treating of all imaginable things under the Zodiac and above it, but of his own personal history only at rare intervals, and then in a most enigmatic manner" (95). The only order in this chaos seems to be that the paper bags in question are each marked with the "symbols of six southern Zodiacal signs, beginning at Libra" (95). On closer inspection of the contents, the editor finds even greater cause for "editorial difficulties" when he discovers an assorted mixture of "Metaphysico-theological Disquisition," "Dreams, authentic or not," "Anecdotes, often without date of place or time," "Washbills," and "Street-Advertisements" (95). By depicting the editor's quandary in dealing with this seemingly irrelevant mass of information, Carlyle singles out the rationalist conception of historicism and treats it as an object of criticism. In response to the editor's pleas for clear historical facts, Teufelsdröckh asks scornfully: "What are your historical facts? Still more your biographical? Wilt thou know a Man . . . by stringing together beadrolls of what thou namest Facts? The Man is the Spirit he worked in; not what he did, but what he became" (100). Carlyle impresses upon us that the historical mode is not primarily a function of the subject. It must be seen as something separate, something on the order of a social convention which must be incurred like a rite in order to preserve the rationalist idea of the self.

The idea of historical consciousness is further undermined by the fact that it relies on the ordering of signs which represent human ideas about essentially mysterious realities. These signs, which stand in for events or experiences which we do not fully comprehend, essentially suppress our primary impression of reality by replacing it with a signified reality. In this sense, the writing of personal history, by raising certain aspects of being to the level of events and experiences while concomitantly ignoring others, finds itself subject to the laws of language and thus closer to fiction than to lived life. It is this affinity between historicity and fiction which tends to push the biographical "I" into the third person, a process which Louis A. Renza calls "writing's law of gravity" (279). We might define this law as the inevitability of a moment of recognition when on hearing one's own narration of the self, one must exclaim, "This is not my life I am talking about!"—when one senses the tension between what one is saying and what is not being included, that moment when the word becomes a precipice over which one discovers a chasm of unacknowledged and inexpressible depth of being. Teufelsdröckh usually refers to himself in the third person, and then never by name. Stressing the connection between history and artistic convention, he says, "Historical Oil-Painting . . . is one of the Arts I never practiced" (199). In other words, historical or biographical writing is an artificial reconstruction of events which, like the trompe l'oeil, projects an illusive depth while at the same time masking a real depth which it becomes the autobiographer's task to explore or to disaffirm.

It is thus essential to Carlyle that the individual recognize that he or she exists within the order of symbols or signs. Teufelsdröckh's biography is a "hieroglyphic truth" in that all outward signs, whether dreams or washbills, are symbols of an essentially mysterious inner being. "It is in and through *Symbols*," writes Carlyle, "that man consciously or unconsciously, lives, works, and has his being" (204). One's happiness or unhappiness is thus based on one's relation to the symbolic order. Like all "terrestial garments," he continues, symbols are subject to "defacement" and "desecration" (210). The only possibility for human salvation lies in revitalizing the symbolic order—in essence, a poetic act which depends upon what Carlyle calls Fantasy, a concept which, much like the Kantian "imagination," transcends rational categories of space and time. Fantasy is for Carlyle the "organ of the Godlike" by which a person, "though based, to all seeming, on the small Visible, does nevertheless extend down into the infinite deeps of the Invisible, of which, Invisible, indeed, his Life is properly the bodying forth" (205).

It is precisely for this reason—the modern recognition that the individual has a certain amount of freedom to reshape the symbolic order into which he or she was born—that, according to Teufelsdröckh, the concept of conversion is available to moderns when it was not understood by the ancients:

> Blame not the word; . . . rejoice rather that such a word signifying such a thing, has come to light in our modern Era, though hidden from the wisest Ancients. The old World knew nothing of Conversion; instead of an *Ecce Homo*, they had only a choice of Hercules. It was a new-attained progress in the Moral Development of man: hereby has the Highest come home to the bosoms of the most Limited; what to Plato was but a hallucination, and to Socrates a chimera, is now clear and certain to your Zinzendorfs, your Wesleys, and the poorest of their Pietists and Methodists. (189)

Carlyle concludes his chapter on symbolism with a call for a new savior of the world, a second Christ, who returns as a poet and maker. "Of this thing, however, be certain: would'st thou plant for Eternity, then plant into the deep faculties of man, his Fantasy and Heart: . . . A Hierarch, therefore, and Pontiff of the World will we call him, the Poet and inspired Maker; who, Prometheus-like, can shape new Symbols, and bring new Fire from Heaven to fix it there" (210).

It would certainly have seemed ironic to the anti-Newtonian Carlyle that his appeal for a new Promethean spirit to revitalize the worn-out symbols of religion should emerge in the twentieth century in the guise of a science of the psyche. If the Christian church in the Victorian period and after had lost much of its power to liberate the individual and had become ever more dogmatic and prohibitive in character, Freudian psychoanalysis seemed to offer a substitute salvational doctrine which, like a more vital Christianity, insisted on a "power not of ourselves that heals." This new self/soul was not only seen as the product of a history, it was also seen as determined by hidden emotions and instincts. It became the self-proclaimed task of psychoanalysis to map this mysterious new terrain and to try to unite the instinctual aspects of human beings with the historical. But behind the nineteenth-century scientistic terminology and the mechanistic metaphors there lurked an undeniably religious character that one could associate not only with the confessional but also with religious rites and mysteries. "Freud," Paul Tillich tells us, "has shown that libidinous elements are present in the highest spiritual experiences and activities of man, and, in doing so, he has rediscovered insights which can be found in the monastic traditions of self-scrutiny as they had been developed in early and medieval Christianity" (53). Bruno Bettelheim criticizes the English translation of Freud's works for creating an unduly analytic and technical rendering of texts, thus obscuring an essentially aesthetic and spiritual character in the original. The very tendency to situate Freud in a religious tradition is itself evidence of both Bettelheim's and Otto Rank's assertions that the modern preoccupation with self or "ego" is nothing more than a secular substitution for a prior preoccupation with the soul.

The parallels between Carlyle's secularized Christianity and the Freudian doctrine of salvation can also be extended. Both Carlyle and Freud characterize the psyche's self-representational ability in terms of a hieroglyphic, or picture, language. Carlyle's image of paper bags filled with assorted fragments and sheets of paper accords well with Freud's view of the unconscious as a palimpsest or rebus which partially reveals and partially hides the mysterious structure underneath. So too, Carlyle's notion that "in the symbol there is concealment and yet revelation," and that "silence and speech, acting together, [create] a double significance" (205–6). Even Carlyle's idea that the human being is enveloped by the symbolic seems to be echoed in Lacan's neo-Freudian "primacy of the signifier." Moreover, Carlyle's adoption of an editor or social "I" seems closely related to Freud's internal "censor," or superego, which pieces together the hieroglyphic memory traces in a way that is acceptable for public view. But of greatest importance is the centrality in both Carlyle and Freud of the conflict between a socially acceptable historical consciousness and a poetic conviction about the inner structuring powers of the psyche. It is this conflict between inner and outer authority which Freud, perhaps more than any modern thinker, tried to reconcile.

For all their differences, the various texts discussed in the previous chapters share at least one important aspect. Each writer has utilized the narrative of conversion to construct and legitimize a satisfactory unity of identity. In each case the use of this totalizing narrative seems to be linked to a transition from one mode of discourse to another, from a language which no longer adequately legitimizes the self to a superior form of authorizing inscription. Augustine's writing does not remain at the level of a confession but finds its ultimate expression in the hermeneutical performance of a "divinely inspired" text. Montaigne, by contrast, relocates the idea of authority in human reason, thus undermining the hieratic conception of "life as language." The most suitable vehicle for this mode of discourse is the essay. Sade pushes the demotic way of thinking much further than Montaigne by using reason first to destroy all hopes for a moral center and, second, to justify his own inconsistent and brutal acts. The importance of Sade in this scheme lies not in the fact that he succeeded in imposing his inner urges on others physically but that the eighteenth-century interest in aberration and pornography gave him the means to establish his authority in writing. This is the root of the modern autobiographical impulse—to confess not in order to be forgiven by another but to construct a confession in such a way that one is oneself the creator and author of one's own absolving authority. Autobiography at this level achieves the double effect of a self-absolution and a "sadistic" authoritarian inscription on others (the reading public) of one's own truth. Rousseau's *Confessions* becomes the paradigm for this combination of salvation and self-justification, creating an imaginary metafather image to overrule other forms of social authority.

The works of De Quincey and Carlyle can be understood as attempts to reinvigorate and reauthorize this metafather fiction through the use of more sophisticated models of subjectivity. The transformation in self-writing reflected in these and other works involves a recognition of the insufficiency of the demotic conception of language and of the necessity of reinfusing the rational spirit with the full resonance and complexity of poetic and hieratic consciousness. Nineteenth-century "poetic" autobiography prepares the way for a new kind of reader whose emergence is embodied, most notably, by the Freudian enterprise later to be idealized in the projection of the secular confessional fantasy as the Lacanian "subject that knows."

It is no coincidence, then, that psychoanalysis began with *The Interpretation of Dreams.* In what he considered his seminal work, Freud attempted to capture the affective reality of the dream at the descriptive and analytic level, not according to a particular codebook—for that would be a return to a hieratic form of expression (and, naturally, the code could vary from one dreamer to the next)—but according to a set of scientific laws governing the origin of all codes and scripts, a set of tropelike functions which described the workings of the psyche itself. The dream, Freud argued, was the representation to "waking man" of an unconscious wish. This wish represented the "drowned body," the culmination of the effects of repression (social inscriptions) on the body. The task of psychoanalysis was to reveal to consciousness the meaning of this wish and to show how culture conspired to suppress it. As in the primitive initiation, although through completely different means, it was an attempt to standardize the dream for everyone.

II

A Matter of Life and Death in the Psyche: Incorporating the Freudian Paradigm

CHAPTER 5

Authorizing the Self in Joyce's *Portrait*

When Joyce abandoned his autobiographical project *Stephen Hero* in favor of the more "aesthetically wrought" *Portrait*, he did not merely consign the notion of a conventional autobiography to the fire, he forged in his own creative fires a portrait of his own becoming. At issue was the very notion of how this identity of self came into being, its *Bildung*, and how this identity might be legitimized as a unified construct. In the earliest sense of the word, *Bildung* involved making oneself into the unified image/portrait (*Bild*) of a divine Author. Although, structurally, *Portrait* seems to follow this pattern in imitating the Christian convention of the conversion narrative, we assume that Joyce is using this convention ironically in order to emphasize his protagonist's disaffection with Catholic authority and to relocate Stephen Dedalus's own authority in a theory of aesthetic production. We also are aware, however, that through his conception of the artist-god, Stephen projects an authorial identity which would simulate the effect of a transcendent authority. In so doing, he illustrates perfectly what Paul de Man formulated as the central problem of reference in autobiography. The question he asked was whether autobiography only creates "the illusion of reference" and is "no longer clearly and simply a referent at all but something more akin to a fiction which then, however, in its own turn, acquires a degree of referential productivity" (69). The real turning point in the work, which is centered on Stephen's well-known vision of the "bird girl," involves the (re)authorization of an aesthetically produced self through a language sanctioned by a new form of transcendental life.

The recognition that a rational, historical account could not in itself legitimize a unity of subjectivity led to the crisis of authority at the turn of the century which affected the major writers of the period and which we have come to associate with the Freudian project. As early as 1897 Freud wrote to his good friend Fliess that "where the unconscious is concerned it is impossible to distinguish between truth and emotionally charged fiction" ("Freud to Fliess" 260). Freud's early recognition of the priority of fantasy in the psyche led him on a lifelong quest to develop a model of the psyche which would account for these "fictionalizing" tendencies, a quest which, according to Jacques Derrida, ended in the "breakthrough" of a psychic writing machine ("Scene of Writing" 73). The problem for Freud, as it seems to have been for writers like Joyce, was not merely that of distinguishing between fact and fiction in autobiographic anamnesis; it was also a recognition of the insufficiency of these conceptions as far as the relationship of consciousness to memory was concerned. If truth was no longer grounded in a chronological rehearsal of the "facts," by what other means—religious, philosophical, or scientific—could the self be validated?

In a concept of autobiography as "referential production," it seems only fitting that in Joyce's *Portrait* the ties between autobiography and confessional writing reemerge. Paul Jay very aptly links Joyce's novel to the conversion narrative: "Thus, while narratives like . . . *Portrait* seek to recount their authors' 'conversion' . . . to a literary career, it is the act of composing those narratives that most crucially helps to enact it" (124). Unlike Stephen's failed conversion to a religious vocation, however, his ultimate conversion to an aesthetic sensibility cannot rely on a given religious authority and its social or ecclesiastical affirmation in the text. Instead it must rely on an alternate structure of authority which Joyce creates through an intricate interweaving of religious and poetic images that link the various stages of Stephen's life teleologically as well as causally in a movement toward its projected resolution.

Despite its complexity, this strategy follows a similar pattern of death and rebirth typical of rites of passage. In this sense Richard Ellmann's summary of the novel as a process of birth is not altogether inappropriate (*James Joyce* 307). But the metaphor is apt only as metaphor, that is, birth as an initiatory process—a rebirth—connoting death to the old self, repression of original desires, and reorientation of original aims. Stephen's development does not follow the gradual, steady growth of a developing fetus but is marked by disruption and discontinuity, by pain and loss. The image of the word "foetus" engraved on a school desk in a classroom of his father's alma mater reminds us that Stephen's own education recounts not the birth but the misbirth of a soul into an environment for which it was not fit.

The gestation of Stephen's soul to which Ellmann refers is linked to Stephen's growth in the use of language, from the naive and frightened child pondering the words of his elders and playmates, to the guilty youth terrorized by the language of conscience, to the defiant young man who wants to "forge in the smithy of his soul the uncreated conscience of his race" (*Portrait* 252–53). The rebirth of Stephen's soul into language is, according to Jay, a threefold process, beginning with the discovery that "words exist in and of themselves as sensuous objects" and that "by associating and linking them together, we in effect create our own world" (128). Later, after his first attempt at writing poetry, Stephen also discovers that there is a "therapeutic kind of relationship between language and the self" (133). Finally, Stephen discovers that language offers him the possibility of freedom by allowing him "to forge for himself his own authoritative voice" (133). But before this authoritative voice can be achieved, Jay continues, "he must first detach himself from a constraining relationship to figures of authority of his past, a detachment that is preceded by his break with their language and with the rhetoric of authority" (134). It is in this last sense, as Jay points out, that although *Portrait* may be metaphorized as a womb in which the gestation of Stephen's soul occurs, it is also the proving ground of his struggle for authority. Like a primitive initiation, which often requires confinement, deprivation, and mutilation, Stephen's development involves a confrontation with authority on several levels—familial, religious, national, and linguistic. Stephen may appear to be in the process of becoming "his own mother," as Ellmann puts it, but, as Jay argues, in order to give birth to his new identity, he must attempt to break down the "legal fiction of paternity," in effect, becoming his own father (139).

The two ideas are not incompatible, however. In the sense that rebirth involves an initiatory process into society in conformity with the cultural rules of that society, it must be understood as an appropriation of the idea of childbirth in the name of the father. The legitimacy of the natural activity of birthing is transferred to that of cultural interactivity through a process of metonymic reconfiguration. As in the traditional process of *Bildung*, a transcendental signifier of cultural authority (i.e., the father) must be invoked at some point in order to ground the identity of self within the artificial womb of culture. As we have seen in the previous chapter, this process of rebirth has involved a continuous reweaving of the linguistic ground of authority in order to recontain and legitimize human desire within the social structure. This grounding activity, it was seen, is essentially a work of language, an attempt to maintain a transcendental signified at the center of cultural articulation that will generate vital links between individual identity and social authority. If a rational historicism failed to achieve this authority in its own right, it was necessary to relegitimize the old narrative forms through new metaphysical means.

Ramon Saldivar argues that Stephen's attempt to replace a Christian transcendental signified with an aesthetic theory is really nothing but this process of relegitimization, a way of substituting one kind of metaphysics for another (192). By creating a form of idealism that can artificially unify the disparate moments of his experience in a vision of harmony and wholeness, Stephen may seem to escape from the net of Christian transcendence, but he becomes entangled in a metaphysical net of his own making. Moreover, Joyce, as "author" of *Portrait*, is not fully exempted from this indictment. According to Saldivar, although Joyce may "strive to keep signification outside the self-presence of transcendental life, . . . the rhetoric of his texts . . . always seems to posit the existence of a transcendental referent, which might serve as the organizing point for all valuative, ethical, and aesthetic judgements" (192). By revealing a necessary, even ontological, connection between the author and his handiwork, Saldivar places us in the uncomfortable position of indicting Joyce for the shortcomings of Stephen's own apparent naïveté.

Because Saldivar's deconstructive analysis functions primarily as an exposé, however, it does not fully account for the complexity of Joyce's peculiar brand of metaphysic. In a move which, as I will argue, reifies the Freudian enterprise, Joyce inverts the notions of presence as an article of religious faith by reestablishing it as a form of psychic writing. He achieves this inversion by weaving an elaborate network of figures drawn from philosophy, myth, ethology, religion, and, of course, psychoanalysis, producing a pseudoaesthetic which is really a theory of perception, or "apperception."

The figural grounding of Stephen's aesthetic is organized primarily around the metaphor of the Egyptian writer-god Thoth. As Saldivar asserts, "In *Portrait*, the figure of Thoth represents the mythical possibility of the creation of a universal language which would communicate the Word of truth and which would be sanctioned by divine, supreme authority" (212). But Saldivar goes on to argue, following Jacques Derrida, that the Thoth myth itself does not support this sanction, since writing only "contingently appropriates the properties of the Father, who is the supreme origin of the authoritative word." Thus, the actual myth would seem to undercut the very purpose for which it was employed. While I agree that Joyce ultimately fails to break free from the transcendental net, I think Saldivar does not fully appreciate the subversive characteristics of Joyce's accomplishment. Neither does he fully take into account Derrida's argument for the more radically subversive function of Thoth within the logocentric tradition. I want to show how Joyce's figural grounding of Stephen's aesthetic ties in with Derrida's argument about the Freudian *machine à écrire* and supports the subversive aspects that Derrida ascribes to Thoth.

Although named only once in Joyce's text, Thoth appears to function as a knot in which several representations of the deity connect in various ways to the narrative as a whole. But when we try to untangle the mythological associations that each of these images represents, we discover, as Derrida does, that "Thoth had several faces, belonged to several eras, lived in several homes" ("Plato's Pharmacy" 86). According to Derrida, the moon and ibis images of Thoth were attempts to subordinate and disguise the god's essentially disruptive nature, a subordination which was adapted in turn by Plato to the Greek conception of logos. In the *Phaedrus*, Plato follows the mythological strand in which Thoth was believed to be the son of the sun-god Ammon-Ra. The moon image thus constitutes that derivative light which replaces the sun-god's superior illumination during his absence:

> One day while Ra was in the sky, he said: "Bring me Thoth," and Thoth was straitaway brought to him. The Majesty of this god said to Thoth: "Be in the sky in my place, while I shine over the blessed of the lower regions. . . . You are in my place, my replacement, and you will be called thus: Thoth, he who replaces Ra." Then all sorts of things sprang up thanks to the play of Ra's words. He said to Thoth: "I will cause you to embrace (ionh) the two skies with your beauty and your rays" and thus the moon (ioh) was born. Later, alluding to the fact that Thoth, as Ra's replacement, occupies a somewhat subordinate position: "I

> will cause you to send (hob) greater ones than yourself—and thus was born the Ibis (hib), the bird of Thoth." ("Plato's Pharmacy" 89)

The moon and the ibis symbols thus appear to be conferred after the fact by Ra, designating Thoth's role as replacement and supplement in the case of the moon, and, as if by way of consolation, providing an assurance of future upward mobility ("greater ones than yourself") with the symbol of the Ibis. Derrida is not convinced: "Once again here we encounter a hidden sun, the father of all things, letting himself be represented by speech" ("Plato's Pharmacy" 87). The aforementioned mythological disguises seem to confirm Derrida's indictment of Western logocentrism. There are too many elements in the mythology surrounding Thoth, he argues, which present him as a destabilizing, volatile force, too powerful to be relegated to any form of subordination for long: "One would be tempted to say that these [characteristics] constitute the permanent identity of this god in the pantheon, if his function were not precisely to work at the subversive dislocation of identity in general, starting with that of theological regality" ("Plato's Pharmacy" 86).

We may therefore ask ourselves just how the various images of Thoth in *Portrait* create a network of subversion in order to "dislocate" Stephen's identity from the constraints of his culture. Curiously, Thoth is invoked precisely in the place where we would expect to find the name Stephen inherits from his father—Dedalus. The substitution evokes a portentous new allegiance of which he is becoming vaguely aware: the image of an unknown and primal father which designates the future world of his longing. "A sense of fear of the unknown moved in the heart of his weariness, a fear of symbols and portents, of the hawklike man whose name he bore soaring out of his captivity on osierwoven wings, of Thoth, the god of writers, writing with a reed upon the tablet and bearing on his narrow ibis head the cusped moon" (*Portrait* 225). At this point, Ellmann observes, the Daedalian image no longer suffices, and Stephen must condense it with other, more fruitful symbols (*Consciousness of Joyce* 17).

The shift from Daedalus to the Egyptian moon-god Thoth, god of writers, is a natural one. The theme of flight is preserved in the Egyptian name and most common hieroglyphic symbol for the god: Tehuti—the ibis—an image which invests its significance retroactively in the names of Stephen's friends Cranly (Crane) and Heron and which becomes condensed into Stephen's vision of the bird girl. The moon image, moreover, is associated at least once with Stephen's relation to his father, intimating Stephen's perceived priority to him and his friends: "His mind seemed older than theirs: it shone coldly on their strifes and happinesses and regrets like a moon upon a younger earth" (*Portrait* 95). The inverted relation between father and son seems to be further borne out by Stephen's relationship to his paternal name. If the meaning which the Greeks eventually attached to Daedalus was "to work with skill," the very archetype and origin of all human skill and artifice is Thoth. Indeed, Thoth even better represents Stephen's forward-looking origination, since Thoth and not Daedalus represents the vocation Stephen chooses. Thoth, moreover, is said to belong to the very oldest conceptions of Egyptian theogeny and may have been adapted from an even earlier stage of civilization or primitive race (Budge 404). He was considered to be the very mind and heart of Ra himself, the god of temporal and spatial measurement, of writing, of human intelligence, and of all arts and sciences, including alchemy and magic. He was also the founder of all moral and civil law, the arbiter of disputes and oppositions, the "all pervading, and governing, and directing power of heaven and earth"—in short, as Egyptologist E. A. Wallis Budge sums it up, a "feature of the Egyptian religion which is as sublime as the belief in the resurrection of the dead in a spiritual body, and as the doctrine of everlasting life" (415).

Indeed, Thoth also played a crucial part in the rebirth of souls as arbiter of the dead. Called the weigher of words, he assumed the role of the recording angel who in a sense held the "dread book of accounts" in his hands, determining whether a soul would enter Sekhet-Hetepu (the Elysian Fields) or remain behind in an eternal death. As the scribe of the gods, he possessed powers greater than those of Osiris or even Ra himself. In his function as writer of all books and controller of all language, his powers were associated with the weaving of a net which held certain souls back while allowing others to pass. In this respect we find a connection to the net symbology used by Stephen in *Portrait*. "The soul is born, he said vaguely, first in those moments I told you of. It has a slow and dark birth, more mysterious than the birth of the body. When the soul of a man is born in this country there are nets flung at it to hold it back from flight.

You talk to me about nationality, language, and religion. I shall try to fly past those nets" (203). It is not inappropriate, then, that Thoth's temple is called the temple of the net. We are told in *The Book of the Dead* of a net which exists in the underworld and which the soul of the deceased regarded with horror. To escape entrapment in this net, the individual was obliged to learn the names of each of its parts, to learn to make use of it, as Budge tells us, "to catch food for himself instead of being caught 'by those who laid snare's" (406). So too, Stephen's escape from the net of the authoritative language of nationality and religion depends on his ability to learn its names, to learn to use the net of language for his own purposes. Stephen's attempt to weave an authoritative power through language can be equated with the prayerful supplications which the ancient Egyptian makes to Thoth so that his dead self/soul may undergo a rebirth in the underworld:

> Hail, thou "god who lookest behind thee," thou "god who has gained mastery over thine own heart," I go a-fishing with the "cordage of the uniter of the earth" . . . and of him that maketh a way through the earth. Hail, ye fishers that have given birth to your own fathers, who lay snares with your nets, and who go round about in the chambers of the waters. Take ye not me in the net wherewith ye ensnared the helpless fiends, and rope me not in with the rope wherewith ye roped in the abominable fiends of the earth, which had a frame which reached unto heaven, and weighted parts that rested upon the earth. (Budge 406)

Significantly, Thoth is referred to as a "self-begotten god," "Lord of Khemennu, self-created, to whom none hath given birth, god 'One' " (400). Through the power obtained by a mastery over the net of language, the writer/supplicant is able to give birth to his own fathering authority.

Stephen's reference to escaping the net also recalls his difficult association with the church and with his Catholic education; St. Peter is the fisher of men, and St. Francis Xavier, patron saint of Stephen's college, is referred to as "a great fisher of souls" (108). Joyce's use of a religious symbolism that reverses the Christian doctrine reveals the subversive function of Joyce's figural design. Outside of *Portrait*, moreover, in the "Hamlet" chapter in *Ulysses*, Stephen makes further references to the self-engendered self—"He who himself begot"

(197), or "himself his own father" (208). These references, reinforcing Stephen's ties to the Egyptian writer-god, also proclaim his heretical relation to the Christian church. As Weldon Thornton indicates, this identification of the father with the son must be linked to the Arian and Sabellian heresies in the early church in which the Father, the Son, and the Holy Spirit were seen not as three persons but as purely different modes of the divine substance. St. Thomas Aquinas describes them much more precisely in his discussion of "Whether the Son is Other than the Father": "Now, in treating of the Trinity, we must beware of two opposite errors, and proceed cautiously between them—namely, the error of Arius, which placed the Trinity of Substance with the Trinity of persons; and the error of Sabellius, who placed the unity of persons with the unity of essence" (*Summa theologica* I, q. 31).

From the point of view of the church, if Stephen is negotiating his passage between this heretical Scylla and Charybdis, he is navigating dangerously nearer to the error of Sabellius's "unity of essence" than the Arian "trinity of substance." But what is considered a heresy in Christian theology appears to have been a credit to the Egyptian writer-god, who was called "thrice-great," a factor which, as Budge notes, was well understood by the Greeks when they called their own equivalent to Thoth "Hermes Trismegistus."

In order to expose the hidden, subversive aspects of the god of the signifier, we might push even further in our genealogical game of symbols which designates the god of writing, and which also forms the outline of Stephen's own struggles with the "signifying net." To the god Hermes the Greeks attributed not only all production of human intelligence and language but also the founding of a system of theology and the organization of a settled government in the country (Budge 414). Here we find Thoth's control over language and reason becoming equated with the logos of Plato (Burkert 40), the very conception of a unity in language which we can relate to the appearance of ideology and the conception of conversion. According to Derrida, Thoth thus became further confined within the logocentric enclosure which founded Western philosophy. And yet it is precisely that disruptive element which, in the very process of its suppression, appears to have been preserved in a symbolism which spanned the ancient world to become part of modern signifying exchange, even to the extent that it informs so much of Derrida's own work.

Even the Greeks were hard put to explain and not a little embarrassed about the symbol of the herm, which Walter Burkert describes as "a rather dignified, usually bearded, head on a four-cornered pillar and, in due place, an unmistakable, realistically molded, erect phallus" (39). These phallic signposts, placed in courtyards and at entrances, were erected (in the most literal sense) to ward off danger and evil spirits. Apollodorus refers also to bedposts in the form of herms as a measure against frightening dreams (Burkert 40). Herms are generally considered apotropaic in nature, that is, fulfilling a function in which an organism or a part of an organism was directed toward an external stimulus for the purpose of repelling. Burkert is unable to find any explanation for the existence of the herm except within the realm of ethology. "There are species of monkeys, living in groups, of whom the males act as guards: they sit up at the outposts, facing outside and presenting their erect genital organ. This is an 'animal function' in the sense noted above: the basic function of sexual activity is suspended for the sake of communication; every individual approaching from the outside will notice that this group does not consist of helpless wives and children, but enjoys the full protection of masculinity" (40). Enjoys the full protection of masculinity! I am reminded here of Rousseau's reference to his adolescent exhibitionism, which he interprets for us as the timid youth's means of enticement. If we are to include this explanation, it would seem that the phallus/herm has at least two interdependent levels of signification: a literal one which points to the function of the body part as an agency of "self"-pleasure, and a "higher" metonymic signification for masculine aggressiveness as an agency to ward off those to whom it means rivalry and aggression.

The ethological explanation proves to be reinforced by the fact that the very earliest references in hieroglyphics to Thoth associate him with the particular species of baboon (*Papio hymadrias*) in which this form of signification has been observed. Budge tells us that these archaic representations of Thoth "take us back to a very remote period when supernatural powers were assigned to the particular class of ape which was the companion of Thoth" (404). But further ethological investigation proves this monistic phallocentric explanation of language to be an oversimplification. For within the "higher" level of signing functions of these particular species, we find that both male and female forms of exhibitionism together fulfill a more complicated function of pacification and repulsion. Specifically, if the phallus/herm fulfills an apotropaic function at the periphery of the hermetic circle, the exhibition of the female genitalia performs a complementary, ameliorative function, disarming rather than warding off aggression, making coexistence within the circle possible. Moreover, these signing functions must be understood as belonging to both sexes. In other words, nature has provided the appropriate markings and genital development to allow either sex to exhibit both signs. If even at the level of nature these two forms of signification are not gender specific (although they are identified with gender), this must certainly apply to language. The problem of phallocentrism in language is not that it excludes the feminine form of signification (for it very much relies on it) but that it sublates it by disguising it within the dialectical field of its own antithesis. The phallus, then, is posited metonymically as a symbol of a total relation, when in fact it is only a part of a dialectical relation that determines individual identity and the place of this identity in the cultural exchange. One of the functions of the Thoth myth in *Portrait* may therefore involve the appropriation and synthesis of cultural determinants of sexual difference, giving the artist the hermaphroditic function of self-procreator, in order to rewrite its own myth of origination.

Such speculation is supported by a profusion of images of creation in *Portrait* associated with the hermetic tradition. Joyce was keenly interested in the symbols and ideas of hermeticism and borrowed extensively from its concepts and image repertoire. In *Portrait* images of light and darkness, of life emerging from chaos, of the cataclysmic and sexual nature of creation, and of the elevation of the human being to that of "mortal deity" all reflect the cultural "antimatter" of hermeticism in Western thinking. This tie to hermetic thought is perhaps most apparent in Stephen's concept of the artist-god, which, as in the hermetic tradition, raises the human to the level of "mortal god." In the hermetic tradition, moreover, the link between humans and god is unmediated and direct. As the messenger god, Hermes reveals himself to humanity through artistic and religious impulses. Unlike the Christian tradition, in hermetic thought nature and humankind are unextricably bound to one another. The "fall," which Stephen eventually recognizes as his destiny, is thus considered a necessary part of the process of enlightenment and salvation. Most significant, however, the hermetic deity is hermaphroditic and, unlike the Judaic or Christian father-God, does not create the world out of nothing but is continually involved in the process of re-creating a world as it perpetually tends toward dissolution.

The central symbol of Hermes—the phallus—must therefore be understood in Lacan's sense as a symbol of a relation between male and female forces. The meaning we can attach to the link between the phallus and the signifier—or, as Lacan would have it, to this signifier of signifiers—is revealed in the very nature of writing itself. As a form of exclusion, writing creates a space for itself in which it affirms its own set of verities at the expense of others; as a form of pleasure/enticement, it offers aesthetically satisfying constructions by which it draws others into its encompassing net. Autobiography, in the primordial sense that I want to give it, as a form of exhibitionism identified by a signifier for a space which it designates as self, is the apotropaic/tropaic narrative par excellence. It is a hermeneutical activity in the most literal sense of the word, a self-begetting relation of consciousness to memory in which the primary communicative functions of attraction and repulsion are fulfilled. Heidegger's etymological acuteness shows us just how Hermes/Thoth is implicated in such a transcription, characterizing Hermes' message as a "playful thinking that is more compelling than the rigor of science" (*On the Way to Language* 29) and associating it with its primal source: "Hermes brings the message of destiny; *hermeneuein* is that laying open of something which brings a message, insofar as what is being exposed can become message" (*Unterwegs zur Sprache* 121–22; trans. Richard Palmer, *Hermeneutics* 13). What *Portrait* reveals about Joyce/Stephen must be interpreted in terms of a forward-looking exposition, a "playful thinking" founded on an underlying mnemonic reality which, if not necessarily borne out by fact, forms a referential "truth" against which all subsequent experience must be interpreted.

CHAPTER 6

Freud's "Magic Slate" and Stephen Dedalus's Aesthetic

If Joyce's novel links modern subjectivity to a mythology of *arch-écriture*, Freudian metapsychology provides us with its theoretical paradigm in the metaphor of the "writing machine." Indeed, it is no coincidence that Derrida identifies both the myth of Thoth and Freud's theory of the psychic writing machine as conceptions in the history of thought which put the "logocentric enclosure" at greatest risk. According to Derrida, Freud "makes of psychical writing so originary a production that writing such as we believe to be designated in the literal sense of the word—a script which is coded and visible 'in the world'—would only be its metaphor" ("Scene of Writing" 73). What the psyche produced in dreams, for example, did not follow a codebook, at least not the fixed codebook that many dream interpreters had proposed. Instead, it produced its grammar from the "inside," from the relations within the spacings and differentiations provided by the memory, an originary language which Freud often associated with ancient hieroglyphics.

> It seems to us more accurate to compare dreams to a system of writing than to a language. In fact, the interpretation of a dream is thoroughly comparable to the deciphering of an ancient figurative script, such as an Egyptian hieroglyphics. In both cases, there are elements which are not determined for interpretation or reading, but, in their role as determinatives, are there simply in order to assure the intelligibility of other elements. The ambiguity of different elements of a dream has its counterparts in these ancient systems of writing. . . . If until now this conception of dream production has not been exploited, it is because of a situation which is easily understandable: the point of view and body of knowledge with which a linguist would approach the subject of dreams are totally alien to the psychoanalyst. ("Claims" 177)

As Freud noted in "The Antithetical Meaning of Primal Words," the ambiguity found in dreams could also be found in language; ancient Egyptian was particularly bountiful in words containing antithetical meanings (156–57). The psyche, Freud argued, would have to produce just such a language which could reveal and conceal at the same time, since the meanings it produced had to satisfy the requirements of the internal forces which motivated the writing and a repressive, socially determined ego which needed to interact with the outside world. Although the dreamwork therefore contained the key to its own meanings, it did not necessarily insist on its discovery and use.

Derrida argues that Freud's analogy of the mystic writing pad fulfilled precisely these requirements of visibility and invisibility through which the constitution of self-consciousness becomes possible. The mystic pad, made up of a protective transparent sheath, a thin piece of wax paper, and a thick slab of resin or wax, is an apparatus which receives the impressions of a stylus on the outside but which makes these impressions visible from the inside by the contact between the wax paper and the slab. Pull the sheath and the wax paper away from the slab, and the "writing" disappears, leaving only a barely visible trace of itself on the slab, which "is legible in suitable lights" ("Note" 230). Thus, the perceptual system itself (the protected wax paper between the sheath and slab) can receive impressions from the inside or the outside, remaining perpetually fresh and clear for its external contact while retaining its ties to the mnemonic traces engraved in the tablet as on a palimpsest.

For Freud, the double-sided nature of the "magic slate" made it the perfect metaphor for the operation of the mind. Years before the idea of a writing machine occurred to him, he had begun to set forth the principles by which the system of combined perception, consciousness, and memory might function. In the final chapter of *The Interpretation of Dreams*, for example, he outlines in a few paragraphs his hypothesis for the development of the psyche on the basis of a phylogenetic speculation (564–68). According to Freud, the perceptual component of the mental apparatus had evolved for defensive purposes, making it initially little more than a simple reflex apparatus. But life's "exigencies" necessitated a further development by which the organism sought not only to avoid pain but to respond to its internal "somatic" needs. The fulfillment of an internal need would be further enhanced by the evolution of mnemonic powers capable of reproducing reliable images corresponding to objects that would satisfy that need. But this development would result in a further complication: how could the psyche control the reproduction of mnemonic images so they would not interfere with the very real business of satisfying needs? In other words, what would keep such a mechanism from hallucinating itself to death? The inhibition of this internal imaging would necessitate the development of another system which would control voluntary motor activity, translating mnemonic traces into the thought processes, which would lead to successfully coordinated activities for satisfying needs. This more-involved thought activity, to which Freud gave the name "preconscious," was a roundabout substitute for the original wishful impulse, a highly differentiated and deferred wish to be sure, in which external contingencies were taken into account. Dreaming, then, was nothing more than a return to the archaic plan, an attempt to "go by the short path" rather than the roundabout way during a time when the phylogenetically "younger" mechanism that controlled motor activity was at rest.

In *Beyond the Pleasure Principle*, Freud draws on Kant's theorem that our notions of space and time are internal, a priori constructs, suggesting further that in a psychoanalytic model of the mind these "necessary forms of thought" would have to manifest themselves in systems closest to the "outer surface" of the organism in order to shield its vulnerable parts against the bombardment of external stimuli. The internal mechanisms of the organism, by contrast, worked on entirely different principles which were "in themselves timeless," or at least "the idea of time could not be applied to them" (28). Although the archaic activity of dreaming would have to reproduce those conditions of time and space by which waking consciousness interpreted external stimuli, it had the additional capacity to suspend the rules by which these perceptions were made available to consciousness because it relied on a system of inscriptions already present and accounted for.

Derrida returns to Kant to describe the ways in which these inscriptions are registered and preserved in the mnemonic system of the writing apparatus. Within the structure of the writing tablet one can perceive what Kant describes as three different modes of time: permanence, succession, and simultaneity. Permanence in the sense that memory, like St. Peter's "dread book of accounts," preserves all traces in some form or another. Succession "not only in the horizontal discontinuity of signs, but writing as interruption and restoration of the contact between the various depths of the psychical levels . . . neither the continuity of a line nor the homogeneity of a volume; only the differentiated duration and depth of a stage, its spacing" ("Freud and the Scene of Writing" 111). Finally, simultaneity, in that the dramas played upon this stage appear from the depths into consciousness "through rapid periodic impulses" (Freud, "Note" 231), often presenting several associations at once with no sense of their original chronicity. In other words, the mechanisms by which such dramas are produced appear to operate in a perpetual present. Echoing Freud's famous formula "ontogeny recapitulates phylogeny," Derrida shifts a search for the origins of writing to an archaeology of the human psyche, to the very mechanism by which it becomes possible to constitute a "self" in the strata of memory. Language and its symbolic and structural variations is made possible only by an identical psychic apparatus which exists before such structures and can reproduce them.

At this point, however, we find ourselves trapped in a vicious circle in which language betrays its limitations by postulating its own effect as a metaphor for a machine which produced it. After all, the writing apparatus is only a metaphor for a psyche-as-machine. Can a metaphor transcend its own prescribed boundaries? As Derrida points out, the psyche as a writing apparatus could not run by itself; it is a dead thing, or as Derrida would like to suggest, it is death itself ("Freud and the Scene of Writing" 114). We might recall Freud's speculation on a "death instinct" whose primal function was the reduction of tensions, death being the ultimate reduction. But Derrida suggests that it is the writing system itself and not a specific instinct which fulfills this function. In the conflict between desire and necessity a surplus of libido is always being invested in this system of representation, where it seeks its own fulfillment. The writing apparatus in turn constructs a necessary form of representation out of its available traces, utilizing its expanded categories of space and time in order to alleviate and to placate the initial tension applied to it. Had Freud lived to witness the growth of cybernetics, with its invention of machines more and more closely approximating the workings of the psyche, Derrida argues, he may better have understood the necessary relation between life and death in the psyche. Derrida maintains that it is precisely because of this balancing between a living, desiring force and a dead mechanism of differentiation and deferral that the production of language, of memory, and of understanding is possible. Writing, Derrida points out, is impossible without repression—a deferment of ends, a substitution of goals, a forgetting of original desires, a sublimation of practices through the production of ulterior meaning. All these aspects can be accounted for only through a system of representation as a form of death.

Is it for this reason that Derrida rather offhandedly returns the theme of writing to its most regressive and primitive registers at the end of his text—to its phallic as well as its sadistic nature? What is noteworthy here about this final link is the suggestion that the economics of the body (in this case represented by the masculine signifier)—the drives for sexual satisfaction and self-preservation—are translated through the representational mechanisms into all the symbolic registers of human culture. On this level of displacement and reappropriation, of symbolic death, metaphor continually exceeds its mysterious progenitor.

The success of Stephen Dedalus's attempt to fly past the nets of authority is solely dependent on his ability to create a net of language for himself by which he can entrap others. At the very moment that Stephen is ready to embark on his self-imposed exile, his flight for freedom, he also realizes that this salvation can be achieved only through the fashioning of authority: "I go to encounter for the millionth time the reality of experience, and to forge in the smithy of my soul the uncreated conscience of my race" (*Portrait* 253). With his aesthetic mission thus defined, his final prayerlike invocation—"Old Father, old artificer, stand me now and ever in good stead"—must go out even beyond the mythical figure that is his namesake to a more primal, self-engendered god, one that exists before all gods, who lived even before humans, who is himself the signifier of all signifiers, the metaphor of the system of writing for which he claims responsibility. Stephen's quest for authority is affirmed in this shift from a known to an unknown. The self is no longer trapped in a false order but must constitute itself in the presence of a wholly alien Other which exists before the net, which can be approached only within the deepest recesses of the cavern of the unconscious. At the end of *Portrait*, the style shifts abruptly from the flowing line of artistic consciousness to the discontinuity of the daily diary, the hypomnematization of desire—Stephen's first awkward attempts at flight. During this practice excursis he records the following dream: "A long curving gallery. From the floor ascend pillars of dark vapours. It is peopled by images of fabulous kings, set in stone. Their hands are folded upon their knees in token of weariness and their eyes are darkened for the errors of men go up before them forever as dark vapours. Strange figures advance from a cave. They are not as tall as men. One does not seem to stand apart from another. Their faces are phosphorescent, with darker streaks. They peer at me and their eyes seem to ask me something. They do not speak" (249–50).

The dream represents Stephen's attempt to break from the signifying order into which he was born and situates him within the prior signification of a psychic mechanism. No longer is the dream of salvation formulated on the basis of a preexistent "Word," the law, handed down from father to son or made eternally present by ritual or faith. No longer does freedom depend upon the alignment of the self with the traditions of the community. It is not even dependent upon the democratic ties made possible by the rational appeal to the common history of origins, to the self-evidence of cause and effect. The insight offered by Stephen's dream projects the possibility of a salvation even beyond the traditional and social determinatives. It proclaims a relation with a silent Other ("They do not speak") which demands a response rather than obedience: "their eyes seem to ask me something." The long curving gallery of kings through which Stephen passes, indeed through which the history of civilization has passed, is the hall of idols "that corrupts [the poet] from without and within" (*Critical Writings* 185). The pillars of dark vapor which ascend from the floor are the erroneous libations of men who believe themselves descendants of these kings but who "now are seen in the halls of the courts of justice, with wig and affidavits, invoking in favor of some defendant the laws that have suppressed their royal titles" (168). They are "poor fallen kings, recognizable even in their decline as impractical Irishmen" (168). These are passages taken from a series of lectures Joyce gave in Trieste in 1907, a time when the autobiographical draft of *Stephen Hero* was being commended to the fire out of whose ashes the new fictive "body" of the self in *Portrait* would emerge. "Nations," he begins in one lecture, "have their ego, just like individuals" (154). He continues by forging a cultural history for Ireland which, if not borne out by fact, is important for the symbolic heritage which he has created for Stephen in *Portrait.* Irish culture, Joyce suggests, is linked to the great culture of the Phoenicians, whose "religion and civilization . . . , later known by the name of Druidism, were Egyptian" (156).

Stephen's dream, however, moves beyond "ancient kings" to the mouth of a cave, at once a phylogenetic and an ontogenetic designation, phylogenetic in the sense that the beings that emerge from this cave seem to be prehuman. They are "not as tall as men." They do not seem to know the diverse stratification of human society but exist in a pure, preindividualized state: "One does not seem to stand quite apart from another." Their faces are masklike, as if painted or tattooed—"phosphorescent, with darker streaks," like baboons—with "moonshane" in their faces. They peer at the dreamer as though across the boundaries of time, inquiring only with their eyes. They are without language. But the dream also recapitulates an ontogenetic movement into Stephen's own psyche, for the dream wish itself which arises from the unconscious core can only gaze out from the depths in the form of a question or a riddle. It is this primordial meeting place—the dream—where "eye contact" is restored, a contact which was lost in the gallery of kings: "their eyes are darkened for the errors of men go up before them forever as dark vapours." Within this space the eyes of the self and the self as other (*das aufgehobene Ich*) meet, and the dream of salvation is produced. Here desire writes out its hieroglyphic charades at the threshold of consciousness.

Who, then, is this "thrice-great" precursor, god of time and space, of memory and writing? It would seem that Stephen's aesthetic theory acquires a necessity quite undreamed of if seen purely from the point of view of its Aristotelian and Aquinian associations. To understand the importance of Stephen's speculations, we must read them as his attempt to formulate an aesthetic that functions as a theory of mnemonic or perceptual organization in order to legitimize the idea of himself as a unified subject. F. C. McGrath has recently shown that Stephen's three "necessary phases of esthetic apprehension" closely follow Hegel's dialectical analysis of sense perception, which was based on the Kantian paradigm. Thus, what Stephen calls "wholeness" or "integritas" reflect Kant's category of permanence, since the separation of an image as an object from all other possible objects, the figure from its ground, seems possible only under the condition of permanence. What Stephen calls "harmony" or "consonantia" appears to be directly linked to Kant's "succession," from which we have learned our ideas of cause and effect in time and of the relations between parts in space. Finally, Stephen's notions of "radiance" or "claritas," which McGrath describes as a simultaneity of apprehension of parts and wholes (242), can be linked to Kant's category of simultaneity. What Stephen seems to be describing is a kind of realignment of two systems of writing, a reformulation of identity under the sign of Thoth. But, as in Derrida, it is a hidden god, this time disguised by the signatures of Aristotle and Aquinas.

The valorized role of the artist as mediator between these two writing systems, as well as its link to the Kantian paradigm, are much more clearly laid out in *Stephen Hero.*

> The artist, he imagined, standing in the position of mediator between the world of his experience and the world of his dreams—"a mediator consequently gifted with twin faculties, a selective faculty and a reproductive faculty." To equate these faculties was the secret of artistic success: the artist who could disentangle the subtle soul of the image from its mesh of defining circumstances most exactly and "re-embody" it in artistic circumstances chosen as the most exact for it in its new office, he was the supreme artist. This perfect coincidence of the two artistic faculties Stephen called poetry. (*Stephen Hero* 77–78)

Kant's masterstroke of dividing the concept of the human imagination into two separate faculties—the reproductive and the productive imaginations—thus appears to have had a formative significance for both Freud and Joyce. It was as if Kant were almost prepared to introduce the notion of an unconscious when he defined the reproductive imagination as "a blind but indispensable power of the soul, without which we should have no knowledge whatsoever, but of which we are scarcely ever conscious" (*Critique of Judgement* 152). But apart from setting forth its universal properties as the basis for perception, Kant did not further define the mysterious relationship between this primary and secondary mechanism. In a world which valorized the Cartesian cogito, the separation was an expedient one. The productive imagination, while deriving its "purposiveness" from the "purposeless" reproductive faculty, would have to have a high degree of independence in order to maintain its dominant position in the human scheme. Philosophically, it was perhaps the safest path to take between two worlds, navigated by the less-fallible *Schüppelgang.*

In the case of Joyce, however, as in Freud, precisely this relation is called into question and is reformulated on the basis of an originary writing, a fictional *arch-écriture*, which asserts itself from the inside out in the nature of a dream wish. In the Kantian paradigm, both Joyce and Freud found the means to rescue the idea of the subject from going the way of the Christian metaphysical tradition, which they rejected and which had lost its power to generate social consensus. By positing the self as a purely formal activity rather than a substantive identity linked to a divine origin, Kantian thought offered a concept of subjectivity sufficiently different in kind from that of Christian metaphysics to endow it with a radically subversive, self-legitimizing power. To be sure, Joyce does not completely align himself with the Freudian enterprise. Certainly he disagrees as to who is best able to interpret the formalizing activity of mind—the artist as opposed to the scientist. Like Freud, however, Joyce appears to fall back into the logocentric trap he is trying to escape. By denominating this unity of subjectivity with a proper name—Stephen Dedalus—and authorizing its existence in the name of the self-legitimating Thoth, founder of the artistic imagination, Joyce may be guilty of the Münchhausen-like act of pulling himself out of his metaphysical quagmire by his own imaginary hair. In other words, in *Portrait* we see an ideological sleight of hand in which the idea of a unity of activity becomes misconstrued as a unity of essence. In effect, author and protagonist are *both* conceived as creations of the text, constituting one another reciprocally in order to legitimize their respective existences as unified constructs.

Joyce creates a mirror inversion of the metaphysical world he seeks to overcome. Although he appears to find it necessary to create an authorizing center in the figure of Thoth, it is not a center in the conventional sense of origin or first cause. It *is* a center in Derrida's sense, however, in that it *represents* the limits of the play of signification from a point somewhere outside of the structure it represents. In *Portrait* we see what might be called a movable center—that is to say, a center posited as projected effect of the moment-by-moment limitation of the play of signifiers. Such a "center" is purely a myth, an "afterimage." It exists only in the sense that it metaphorizes an unknown operation which controls the limiting action of a present signifying play. Although it must be recognized as an absence, it always ends up being replaced by a series of interchangeable presences, just as Thoth lets himself be represented by a series of seemingly permanent masks in order to obscure the fluidity, the apparent relativity of play itself. In the final analysis, this ever-changing play of signification is not relative, since it is finite, even historically differentiable—merely not yet finished. There is, in other words, no final analysis, only a series of ongoing prognostications. The final structure is only more complex than can be imagined from any point of play in the signifying game. The constants of the formalizing powers of mind cannot be identified in a continually shifting field of signifiers because there is no metalanguage outside this field with which to identify them. Thus, the job of interpreting these repetitions in flux would better suit the hermetic power of the artist than the rational activity of the scientist.

Might we not therefore sketch as a tentative contour in Freud and Joyce the return of a repressed and dangerous god (from the point of view of the sun) whose attributes, projected as the relational categories of perception itself, form a powerful trinity blasphemous to Western thought, so much so that they must have been suppressed already in Egyptian theogeny and certainly subordinated by Plato, whose proponents were burned at the stake in Christendom and who even today are pilloried in the stocks of a nineteenth-century conception of science and art—in short, an archaic insistence, the return of hermetic thinking, which threatens the continuation of hierarchies and hegemonies, which seeks to undermine the repressive valuations which culture imposes on the internal relations of the individual mind in search of its ultimate freedom and self-mastery?

CHAPTER 7

The Mirror of the Text: Rilke's "Other Self"

IN THE FIRST English edition of Rilke's *Die Aufzeichnungen des Malte Laurids Brigge*, the translators, M. D. Herter Norton and John Linton, dissented from using the original title in favor of *Journal of My Other Self*. As Norton argues in her foreword to a later translation in which she restores Rilke's wording, this initial choice of title, although perhaps too obviously suggestive, was not inappropriate (8). Rilke had often spoken of his "other self" to his friend and confidant Lou Andreas-Salomé. It was because of this other in Rilke, this "too easily depressed, too excitable, too fearful, then again too impetuous" side of him that Salomé feared for Rilke's sanity (*Rilke-Salomé Briefwechsel* 41; trans. mine). In a letter ominously entitled "Last Plea" she explained to him why she had stopped seeing him, that the "other" in him had threatened to destroy her and would surely destroy him if he did not try to save himself (43). Not yet having joined the Freudian circle, her injunction to him took on Nietzschean overtones, "Follow the same path toward your dark god." Rilke's response came almost three years later, and in the letters that followed we find the first autobiographical accounts of Rilke's Paris experience, which, with Salomé's encouragement, were to inaugurate the *Notebook*. As the original title indicates, however, the proper name attached to these initial autobiographical fragments was not Rainer Maria Rilke, the son of a Prague railway official, but Malte Laurids Brigge, the last in a line of two Danish aristocratic families. The question I want to ask is, Who is this fictive other self, this child of a distinguished but imaginary past constructed out of the author's own crisis but mirroring his discontent in a way that his own biography apparently could not? Through this specific inquiry we might also discern an even larger question which we can formulate with the words of Jacques Lacan: "Who, then, is this other to whom I am more attached than to myself, since, at the heart of my ascent to my own identity, it is still he who agitates me?" (*Ecrits* 172).

For Lacan, the question of the other is tied to the "mirror stage" which he posits both as a formative event and as an ontological category. Beginning with the infant's precocious self-recognition as a specular totality (precocious because it does not yet experience its own body as a coordinated unity), the mirror stage initiates the process by which the child first learns to constitute itself as a subject through the internalized imago of another. But Lacan moves beyond the scientism of Freud by shifting his focus onto a study of the unconscious as an effect of language. Although the mirror stage is posited as a prelinguistic event, its importance, for Lacan, lies in the way it sets the stage for the acquisition of language. Thus an essentially alienating experience of the self in the realm of the "imaginary" becomes informed by an equally alien but socializing institution of language, making all further permutations of the imaginary occur within the communal registers of the symbolic. Despite the "primacy" which Lacan thereafter accords to the signifier, however, there remains a level of experience at which the initial imago retains its hold on subjectivity, becoming the primary referent against which all self-referential signifiers are determined. This results in a dialectical relation between two not necessarily compatible mediums, between the coexistence of the image and the temporality of the word, which can be mediated only by the appropriate figures of thought and speech.

In his essay "Autobiography as De-facement," Paul de Man reinforces Lacan's theory when he identifies autobiography with the figure of prosopopoeia—the conferring of a mask or a face. As he sees it, the central problem of autobiography, as a "discourse of self-restoration" (74), is that of translating into the temporality of language a self-recognition which is essentially specular in nature. Insofar as this process involves the conferring of a figurative mask, it also involves a defacement or disfiguration of the very experience it seeks to represent. "How can this harmless veil [of language]," de Man asks, "suddenly become as deadly and violent as the poisoned coat of Jason or of Nessus?" (80). One of Malte Brigge's childhood memories vividly illustrates how the conferring of a face "deprives and disfigures to the same extent that it restores" ("Autobiography as De-facement" 81). Discovering a room full of costumes in his ancestral home, young Malte soon learns the restorative powers of masquerade. "Hardly had I donned one of these suits, when I had to admit that it had me in its power; that it prescribed my movements, the expressions of my features, even, indeed, my ideas. My hand, over which the lace cuff fell and fell again, was anything but my usual hand: it moved like an actor; I might even say that it was watching itself, exaggerated though this may seem. These disguises never, indeed, went so far as to make me feel a stranger to myself: on the contrary, the more varied my transformations, the more assured I was of my own identity" (97).

When he discovers a collection of masks, however, he also learns of the dangers of prosopopoeia. Completely disguised in mask, scarves, and robe, he accidentally knocks over a little table laden with "small fragile objects" which are "shivered into a thousand tiny fragments." To set things aright he frantically turns to the mirror to undo his costume:

> But just for this the mirror had been waiting. Its moment of revenge had come. While I strove with measurelessly increasing anguish to tear myself somehow out of my disguise, it forced me, by what means I know not, to lift my eyes, and imposed on me an image, nay, a reality, an alien, unbelievable, monstrous reality, with which, against my will, I became permeated: for now it was the stronger, and it was I who was the mirror. I stared at this great, terrifying, unknown personage before me, and it seemed appalling to me that I should be alone with him. But at the very moment I thought thus, the worst befell: I lost all knowledge of myself, I simply ceased to exist. For one second I had an unutterable, sad, and futile longing for myself, then there was only he—there was nothing but he. (100)

Malte's recognition and subsequent loss of himself in the image of the other seems to conform to the Hegelian concept of *Aufhebung*, or "sublation," a term which in Hegel means "simultaneous destruction and preservation." Literally defined as "to lift up," the related German word *aufheben* also can mean "to deny," "to remove," or "to disaffirm," but there are also popular connotations such as "to put into storage," "to keep in good hands" (e.g. a child), or "to apprehend" (e.g. a criminal). If, following the Hegelian model, Malte's self "has come outside of itself," this should, according to Hegel, be experienced in two ways. "First it has lost its own self, since it finds itself as an *other* being; secondly, it has thereby sublated that other, for it does not regard the other as essentially real but sees its own self in the other" (Hegel 229). Malte's experience may emulate the initial stage of the Hegelian model, but it does not fulfill the final goal of sublation necessary to "becom[ing] one with itself again" (*Phenomenology* 229–30). Instead, the relation between self and self-as-other undergoes a reversal as Malte's consciousness of himself is overwhelmed and annihilated in the spectacle of the other. Completely suspended (*aufgehoben*) in this condition, Malte can appeal only to the servants (i.e. the Hegelian "slave") to restore him to his former position of self-presence.

> I ran away from him, but now it was he that ran. He knocked against everything, he did not know the house, he had no idea where to go; he managed to get down a stair; he stumbled over someone in the passage who shouted in struggling free. A door opened, and several persons came out. Oh, oh, what a relief it was to recognize them! There were Sieversen, the good Sieversen, and the housemaid and the butler; now everything would be put right. But they did not spring forward to the rescue; their cruelty knew no bounds. They stood there and laughed; my God, they could stand there and laugh! I wept, but the mask did not let the tears escape; they ran down inside over my cheeks and dried at once, and ran and dried again. And at last I knelt before them, as no one has ever knelt before; I knelt, and lifted up my hands, and implored them, "Take me out, if it is still possible, and keep hold of me!" But they did not hear; I had no longer any voice. (100–101)

In the sense that prosopopoeia deprives the autobiographer of a face and a voice in the very act of conferring one, it poses a double threat: that of suffocation (or poisoning, to use de Man's illustration) and that of defacement—of losing one's face altogether. There are, of course, "simple, thrifty folk" who, according to Malte, wear the same face for years, passing on those they did not use to their children. Others, by contrast, use up their faces "in rapid succession," wearing the last one out in a week, leaving nothing behind but the lining, the "no-face." But the ultimate horror is revealed to Malte when he unintentionally startles a woman on the street who is completely "sunk into herself, head in hands": "The woman took fright and was torn too quickly out of herself, too violently, so that her face remained in her two hands. I could see it lying in them, its hollow form.

It cost me an indescribable effort to keep my eyes on these hands and not to look at what had been torn out of them. I shuddered to see a face thus from the outside, but I was still more afraid of the naked, flayed head without a face" (*Notebook* 7).

Malte elaborates on this motif in his later description of two historical figures which, as Rilke once explained, were not meant to be understood historically but as "vowels of Malte's affliction" (*Selected Letters* 391). There is the case of the "false Czar," Grischa Otrepiof, who, killed by a mob after his masquerade had been revealed, was given a mask on his deathbed to hide his "stabbed and mangled" face (177). Or again there is the death of Charles the Bold, duke of Burgundy, whose countrymen attempt to identify his corpse after the battle of Nancy, even if his face, half frozen in the ice, half devoured by wolves, has become completely disfigured. In both cases the constitution of the subject falls into jeopardy because the external relationship conflicts with its internal counterpart, the meaning of which has already been determined in advance. Ironically, in the case of the false czar, it is the real czar's mother who claims to recognize him as her own son and, in so doing, confers on him an identity that leads to his own self-doubt: "Did not his uncertainty begin when she acknowledged him. I am not disinclined to believe that the strength of his transformation consisted in his no longer being the son of anyone in particular" (178).

The case of the duke of Burgundy also projects the significance of this process of self-identification and self-aggrandizement beyond the horizon of a domestic tragedy. A stranger to his own country, speaking English rather than French, identifying himself with his mother's Portuguese background—indeed, recognizing this inheritance in the features of his face and body—the duke has lost his identity long before his friend and confidant the count of Compabasso openly betrays him in battle. Yet his tenuous position of leadership over his subjects cannot be said to be the cause of his downfall. It results from and metaphorizes an internal condition which has worked its way outward from a coexistent, specular truth, which informs all his choices, into the sequentiality of historical event. As an objective correlative of a complex and contradictory internal condition, the mutilated face becomes more valid than the former public visage. His countrymen, like some "referentiality-based" autobiography scholars, may be hard put to identify their man in his state of disfiguration, but according to the duke's fool, they are looking in all the wrong places when they ferret out an ingrown toenail, a small scar, and two ulcers on the neck. As the fool expostulates, "Ah! Monseigneur, forgive them for revealing your gross defects, dolts that they are, and not recognizing you in my long face, in which your virtues are written!" (185).

If the concept of self is founded on the illusion of a specular totality—the face and, by extension, the body—then autobiography becomes the measure of how that illusion is or is not taken up into language. In Rilke's *Notebook* this experience is expressed primarily in terms of fragmentation—in Malte's sense of himself, in his memories, and in the fragmentation of the text itself. Rilke's idea for this fragmented narrative may well have come from his first visits to Rodin's studio, which he described in a letter to his wife. (The letter is addressed and dated "Paris, 11 rue Toullier, Dienstag, 2 September, 1902"; the first journal entry in the *Notebook* is "11 September, rue Toullier.")

> It is indescribable! Nothing but fragments lying, for several meters, one next to the other. Pieces as big as my hand, and bigger . . . but just pieces, hardly anything whole, often just a fragment of an arm, or a leg, carelessly lying next to one another, and a fragment of body to which they belong, nearby. There a torso of one figure with the head of another pressed against it, with an arm of a third . . . as if an immense storm, an unprecedented catastrophe had passed through this work. And yet, the closer you look at it, the more deeply you feel, that everything would be less unified, if the individual bodies were whole. Every one of these fragments is of such an eminent, gripping unity, so *possible* by itself (indeed not thinkable otherwise), that one forgets that they are only parts and often parts of different bodies, they seem so attached to one another. You suddenly feel that it is more the business of the scholar to understand the body as a whole, and much more that of the artist to create new relationships between these fragments, new, greater, more law-abiding unities,—more eternal. (*Briefe, 1897–1914* 34–35; trans. mine)

Rilke's expressions of fragmentation quite clearly can be identified with Lacan's category of the fragmented body, which in his theory of the mirror stage, he raises to the level of a theoretical referent because of its frequent manifestation in analytic practice. The fragmented body represents the anxiety of a being whose primary referent can be neither completely realized nor fully transcended; in the socialized being it establishes the "lines of fragilization" at which the elements of an imaginary totality have become fractured by their reappointment within the signifying chain. It would seem to be no coincidence, then, that both Lacan and Rilke turn to the paintings of the fifteenth-century mystic Hieronymus Bosch in order to express this primordial fear of fragmentation. According to Lacan, this fragmented body "usually manifests itself in dreams when the movement of the analysis encounters a certain level of aggressive disintegration in the individual. It then appears in the form of disjointed limbs, or of those organs represented in exoscopy, growing wings and taking up arms for intestinal persecutions—the very same that the visionary Hieronymus Bosch has fixed, for all time, in painting, in their ascent from the fifteenth century to the imaginary zenith of modern man" (*Ecrits* 4–5). Malte Brigge, by contrast, sees in Bosch's paintings not only the recognition that the body has become caught up in a language which deforms and fragments it but also the possibility of a restoration in their intimation of new, heretofore unimagined relationships.

> How well I understand now those strange pictures in which things meant for restricted and regular uses distend and wantonly touch and tempt one another in their curiosity, quivering with the casual lechery of dissipation: cauldrons that go about boiling over, pistons that have ideas, useless funnels that squeeze themselves into holes for their pleasure! And behold! among them, too, thrown up by the jealous void, members and limbs, and mouths pouring their warm vomit into them, and windy buttocks, offering them satisfaction. (*Notebook* 173–74)

The associations in this vivid description seem to be primarily linked to sexual desire. The "void," that chaos of memory, jealous of the freedoms that other objects enjoy in their associations with one another, releases these members and limbs of the imaginary body from their repressed ("restricted and regular") uses, allowing them to combine with other signifiers in a "discourse of self-restoration."

> And the saint writhes, and shrinks into himself; yet there was a look in his eyes that admitted the possibility of these things: he glanced at them. And already his senses are forming a precipitate in the clear ichor of his spirit. Already his prayer is stripped of its foliage and stands up out of his mouth like a wilted shrub. His heart is overturned and has flowed out into the surrounding turbidity. His scourge falls as weakly upon him as a tail that flicks off flies. His sex is once again in one place only and when a woman comes straight through the huddle towards him, her naked bosom full with breasts, it points towards her like a finger. (174)

Walter Seifert tells us that Malte is alluding to Bosch's depictions of St. Antony, whose renunciation of sensual temptations raises him to the highest stage of human wisdom (181). In one picture, as Charles De Tolnay describes it, the saint's body has "become an insensitive rock; his eyes, the only part of him still alive, gazing with superhuman intensity at the 'things which pass all understanding' " (306). But Rilke does not associate the saint with some "higher state" of celibacy. Instead he seems to be concentrating on a form of renunciation and (re)signation which restores virility and leads to a more focused, "spiritualized" sexuality linked to creativity.

This paradoxical vision of a restored, creative sexuality is evident in Bosch's masterful triptych *The Garden of Earthly Delights*, the right panel of which seems to figure prominently in Malte's description. Here Bosch represents a dream landscape in which objects and human body parts have entered into startling new combinations. The work was initially interpreted by Christian apologists like Joseph de Singuença as a didactic sermon against the lusts of the flesh (837–41). More recently, however, Wilhelm Fraenger has argued for an antithetical viewpoint—namely, that the painting represents the Adamite doctrine of Bosch's day which preached sexual freedom and complete equality between the sexes as the "upward path" (*acclivitas*) to attaining full harmony between the human soul and nature as it was before the Fall (13–25).

Indeed, the picture evokes both a threat of damnation in the terror of the "fragmented body" and a promise of salvation in the fascinating possibility of new associations between the disparate elements. Two images stand out by virtue of their central position and their size. One is an overscale, realistic depiction of a human face, masklike in its lurid intensity. The face appears to be looking back over the shoulder of a grotesque hollow torso containing an inn scene and is topped by a flat disk which supports a huge bagpipe, Bosch's symbol of male sexuality. What is striking about the face is its intense gaze, reminding me of St. Anthony, as if only such a gaze could endure the grotesque spectacle before it. Even so, it is more likely the face of a "sinner," one transfixed by the objects before it, incorporating them and transforming them into a sexual "music" through the bagpipe.

The other focal point, immediately next to these very libidinous looking bagpipes, consists of a pair of gigantic ears affixed to the handle of a huge and threatening knife. The ear-knife apparatus looks like a tank as it crushes people in its path. Furthermore, it has positioned itself dangerously close to the giant bagpipe. In the sense that the fragmented body is related to sexual desire, as it clearly is in Bosch's landscape and in Malte's interpretation, this scene appears to underwrite the Freudian notion of castration. Nevertheless, the category of the fragmented body might be understood as prefiguring the Freudian conception in that it determines the very possibility of castration as an interpretive recourse. Castration anxiety would therefore seem to be the aftereffect of the more primal threat of fragmentation, once desire has acquired a sexual focus and is redefined according to a network of masculine valuations in language. We need not debate the ideological reductiveness of a theory whose central image—the phallus—becomes metonymous for desire. Surely desire, and hence fragmentation, can be experienced and defined in other ways. But if we retain the conception purely as a descriptive term in the case of Bosch, it would seem a rather odd coincidence that the human ear wields the knife and that the human eye absorbs the images of the body and transforms them into "sexualized" music. What kind of hostage crisis is this when the ear holds desire hostage in order to place the eye at its service? Might we not posit a similar relationship in the process of prosopopoeia, in which the imago becomes defaced by the demands of language?

De Man illustrates this translation from sight to sound with the figure of the tombstone in Wordsworth's "Essay upon Epitaphs," defining autobiography as a representation of what can never be more than an absence. Still, we must ask ourselves how this absence manifests itself within the reader's imagination. Here we might consider de Man's formula for autobiography as a "figure of reading" by which "two subjects determine each other by mutually reflexive substitution" (70). In this sense, reading autobiography implies a recovery of an imago by trying on the figurative mask of another, something which would seem possible only if the reader's own specular sense of self becomes implicated in a process of substitution or exchange. At the contractual level of genre this may well involve a pact between a reader and writer, as Philippe Lejeune has defined it (3–30), but as a "figure of reading," it could also be described as a seduction or lure—the lure of the mirror in the text. When we read a work as autobiography, our concern is not with verifying the factuality of the account before us—that seems to be more the business of the scholar. What we are doing instead is to verify at the level of language what we imaginatively experience as our own body, its divisions, its "lines of fragilization." We do this by taking on the imaginary body and mask of another and by playing out Malte's childhood game of masquerade in the mirror of the text. Or, as in Malte's experience, perhaps it is the other way round; perhaps we become the mirrors in which the text reconstitutes itself as image.

A more fitting metaphor for this very serious game of masquerade may therefore be the death mask, made from a plaster cast taken from the face of the deceased, a mask which covers up what it purports to reveal, which renders permanent what is ephemeral, establishes a presence where there is only absence. Malte describes two death masks hanging outside the shop of the plaster-cast maker. One is the mask of a drowned woman, a suicide, cast in the morgue only "because it was beautiful, because it smiled, smiled so deceptively, as though it knew" (*Notebook* 72). According to William Small, this was a famous death mask of the time known in Paris as *La Noyée de la Seine* (24). The other mask, also famous but not simply for its appearance, is none other than that of Beethoven, described by Malte as the one who "did know." "That hard knot of senses drawn tense; that unrelenting concentration of a music continually seeking to escape, the countenance of one whose ear a god had closed that he might hear no tones but his own, so that he might not be led astray by what is transient and confused in sounds, but in whom dwelt their clarity and enduringness; so that only soundless sense might bring in the world to him silently, a waiting world, expectant, unfinished, before the creation of sound" (73). The two masks establish the fundamental division within which language structures every identity, through the dialectic of "seeing" and of "being seen." Within this division, the body is caught up in a plethora of oppositional values. In the sense that the feminine mask is associated with "being seen," it represents beauty, immutability, and harmony, but also muteness, namelessness, deception, and drowning. The masculine mask, by contrast, represents the seeing subject, its knowledge, concentration, and creativity, but also its disfiguration and, above all, its narcissistic deafness, which enables it to transform all the other "silent" senses into its own language of sound. For Malte, these are not ideological considerations. They are the divisions by which his own identity has been transformed and disfigured. They reflect the process of what Julia Kristeva calls "an interiorization of the founding separation of the sociosymbolic contract" (484). For is it not the feminine mask with which Malte most strongly identified, whether she is Joan of Arc or a slave girl in his childhood dress-up games, or Sophie, the little girl he becomes to satisfy his mother's desire, or the many historical and mythical women with whom he identifies as an adult? The feminine mask represents the drowned self within him, the "other" self he has had to repress in order to assume his masculine role.

Malte's description of the two masks and his subsequent eulogy of Beethoven's creative genius sets forth a metaphoric chain by which we can understand the process of prosopopoeia at the intersubjective level. The woman's mask (*La Noyée* — the drowned one), the voiceless image of specular beauty, is (sub)merged into the "seeing subject" (Beethoven) and converted into a temporal flow of acoustic images. The two thereby become one: a double mask. No longer merely the figure of a unified voice beyond the grave, the double mask sets up a dialectic between the voice of the writing, creating self and the hidden silent language of the sublated other self, the drowned body.

At first Malte likens this transmutation from image to voice to a process of condensation in which the various impressions of the silent senses, represented as random rain showers, are invisibly collected out of all things and condensed into a precipitate (an ichor) which domes the heavens and is released as music to replenish the world. Then, however, he shifts the image. This creative rain suddenly becomes the seed which enters the ear and conceives a new body within the womb of the mind. The word becomes flesh, not unlike medieval representations of the immaculate conception which traced the transformation from eye to ear more directly as a ray of heavenly light entering the virgin's ear to become incarnated as Christ. The sexual symbolism, if present there only by implication, becomes fully elaborated in Rilke's text.

Taken literally, this would appear to be a highly narcissistic conception of identity. If, however, we understand this "sexual" dialectic between eye and ear as representing a relation between the self and the self-as-other, we can better grasp the function of this Beethoven-like creativity for Malte. The conditions for reception are already implied in its internal dialectic. As readers of this text, we are judged in advance. And Malte's judgment, like that of some latter-day prophet, is harsh and decisive. Insofar as this "music" leads to an aesthetic appreciation, as we would expect from fiction, it is compared to a masturbatory satisfaction: "The seed streams forth, and they stand under it like sluts and play with it, or it falls while they lie there in their abortive satisfaction, like the seed of Onan amongst them" (73). Yet to the extent that the reader risks his or her own sense of selfhood, which Malte likens to a virginal body, then the mind miraculously creates a new body out of a comingling of elements: "But master, if ever a virginal spirit were to lie with unsleeping ear beside your music he would die of blessedness, or he would conceive the infinite and his impregnated brain would burst with so great a birth" (73).

Malte leaves us little doubt that his conception of Beethoven's music is analogous to the kind of writing to which he aspires, a radically new form of writing which destroys the temporality of language in favor of an expression of simultaneity. "There will come a day when my hand will be distant from me, and when I bid it write, it will write words I do not mean. The day of that other interpretation will dawn, when no word will properly follow another, and all meanings will dissolve like clouds, and fall down like rain. Despite my great fear I am yet like one standing in the presence of great things; and I remember that I often used to feel like this when I was about to write. But this time I shall be written. I am the impression that will transform itself" (50).

This "other interpretation" or, to invert the phrase, this interpretation of the "other" cannot take full effect until all the fragments of the text are present to the reader's mind (like the memory traces themselves) and begin to exert their influence as a coexistent reality. Now that the total field of fragments inhabits the arena of the mind, it becomes involved in a complex exchange of significations with the individual memory. As in Bosch's landscape, the "jealous void" releases its elements (the body) in hieroglyphic fashion to confront the fragments before it. Insofar as the text does not offer us a narrative unity, we begin to impose our own structural associations, privileging certain images over others. The fragmented body of the text makes us determined to project our own sense of specular unity on the disparate elements.

In our interpretative masquerades, we look up from time to time expecting to see the mask of another; to our amazement we do not lose ourselves in this other but, like Malte, seem to confirm, even define, our own identities in the process of masquerade. But then the unexpected happens. Insofar as the fragments resist our reflex for order, we begin to sense an insistent presence somewhere behind the comforting identity we imagine to be ourselves, an agitation, which at times assumes the proportion of panic. Who, then, is this other self who agitates us so in our ascent to our own identities? Perhaps it is that part of ourselves which can be defined only by its absence, a silent and suspended self trapped behind all language, one that sheds tears never seen, one that cries to be let out but is never heard.

CHAPTER 8

Rilke's God

> The drive to produce art is nothing less than the ongoing attempt to neutralize the conflicts that strain and threaten our many faceted and often contradictory self as it continually struggles to reconstitute itself. —Rilke, *Briefe aus Muzot, 1921–26*

IN WRITING THE *Notebook*, Rilke seems to have taken Lou Andreas-Salomé's advice to follow the imaginative path—the path toward his own "dark god"—to save himself from the emotional impasse he had reached. Yet if the process of writing the *Notebook* can be understood as a form of self-therapy, the end result of this process is by no means conclusive. Malte ends his notebook with a revised version of Christ's parable of salvation, the story of the prodigal son, an ending which Herbert Naumann has called the key to the entire novel. In this version Malte concludes that the prodigal has grown beyond the capacity of his family to love, indeed that even the love of God is not yet possible.

Certainly Malte's ambivalence toward a traditional religious salvation reflects Rilke's own reservations about Christianity. Rilke wrote his first love letter to Lou Andreas-Salomé after he had read her controversial essay "Jesus the Jew," in which he saw parallels to his own *Visions of Christ*, a collection of poems which has the figure of Christ repenting of his false teachings. In essence, the poet accuses Christ of setting himself up as a middleman, interfering with the dialogue between the individual and God. It was a work which Rilke wisely withheld from publication and which did not appear until 1959. Yet Malte's revision of the prodigal son story has more wide-reaching implications. The Christian parable of repentance and reconciliation is perhaps the most influential totalizing narrative in Western culture, linking individual identity with a socially sanctioned transcendental authority. In its original form, the parable deals with the generational transfer of authority in a patriarchal culture, establishing a conciliatory alternative to the strict Judaic model of filial obedience and paternal control. In Rilke's text, however, the original function of the myth is completely undermined. Significantly, the father disappears entirely, and the anticipated reconciliation and self-legitimization do not occur. We are thus led to suspect that the totalizing strategy of this salvational narrative is the object of an elaborate critique to be found in the *Notebook*. Thus, instead of focusing, as other interpreters have, on the prodigal son narrative, we may better understand its function by turning our attention away from the ending toward the strategies in the text through which this narrative is undermined.

Indeed, Rilke's reluctance to commit himself to a salvational doctrine is not aimed solely at Christianity. It is also evident in his oedipal representations in the *Notebook*, just as it is in his subsequent rejection of psychoanalysis. Rilke may have shared with Freud the notion that creative expression was a form of self-therapy, but he adamantly refused psychoanalytic help to deal with the many emotional crises that plagued his life. For Rilke, psychoanalysis and art were mutually incompatible; to choose one meant having to repudiate the other, and if it came down to a choice, no matter how miserable he felt, he vowed never to give up writing. A year after the *Notebook* appeared, responding to Lou Andreas-Salomé's suggestion that he undergo therapy, he wrote, "Psychoanalysis is too fundamental a help for me, it helps you once and for all, it clears you up, and to find myself finally cleared up one day might be even more hopeless than this chaos" (*Selected Letters* 197, Dec. 28, 1911). Shortly thereafter, in a letter to psychoanalyst Emil Freiherr von Gebsattel, he again rejected the "once and for all" salvation of the psychoanalysic "cure," preferring his own more dynamic and ongoing conception of salvation through the production of art: "I know things aren't going well with me, and you, my dear friend have noticed it too,—but believe me, I am nevertheless moved by nothing so much as by the incomprehensible, the stupendous marvel of my own being which was so impossibly biased from the start and which yet travelled from salvation to salvation, as through ever harder stone, so that, whenever I think of not writing any more, this fact alone dismays me, the fact of not having recorded the absolutely miraculous line of this so strangely lived life" (*Selected Letters* 197).

The basis for Rilke's rejection of the Freudian model can be traced through a complex set of interrelated figures in the *Notebook*. Significantly, just as in Malte's revision of the prodigal son story, the image of the father seems to be conspicuously absent in Malte's oedipal associations. Thus, in recasting both myths, Malte not only reveals the complicity of the structure of authority in the two paradigms but indicates the possibility of subverting the powerful role of the father in both structures. Both the Christian and the Freudian myth deal with the problem of authority in a patriarchal culture and warn of the inevitable conflicts that arise in the generational transition of this authority. Yet Freud's paradigm goes further in revealing the motivation for the conflict between father and son. In Christ's parable the libidinal incentive for the son's departure and the maternal influence over his return is overdetermined by the assumption of male entitlement. The mother is not named, but at the same time she is represented as landscape, the nurturing farm, the father's possession. The Freudian myth, by contrast, deals more emphatically with the maternal role in the son's return. The mother is designated as origin and metonymy of the son's desire; the father, as the looming impediment to be dealt with along the way.

In Rilke's text both salvational paradigms are associated with different mediums. The Christian paradigm, with its emphasis on the father, retains a narrative structure; the oedipal associations, by contrast, with their emphasis on the mother, seem to be primarily linked to a specular order. Thus the novel's apparent lack of narrative structure provides us with a starting point in understanding Malte's relation to the Christian narrative of return and reconciliation. Made up of seventy-one diary entries, or "fragments," as Rilke called them, the work resists efforts to interpret it in terms of a narrative unity. Indeed, some critics have concluded that the compositional structure of the *Notebook* puts the very function of narrative as a unifying agency in question. Ulrich Fülleborn, for example, argues that Rilke's novel both destroys the old laws of narrative form and either creates or anticipates a new form of artistic consciousness (161). However, whereas Fülleborn links this new form of consciousness to the associative language of music, the very title of the work—*Aufzeichnungen*, which derives from the verb *zeichnen*, "to sketch"—suggests that the organization of the text is based on a specular model.

Rilke's rejection of a definitive narrative order might well be understood as having an ideological dimension. As previously argued, the central problem of the autobiographical consciousness is that of translating into the temporality of language a self-recognition which is essentially specular in nature. If we are to understand the autobiographical process in de Man's terms as a "de-facement" or "dis-figuration," we can delineate the ideological implications of such a translation. Through the acquisition of language, that "alienation into the signifying chain," the experience of unity or disunity comes to depend almost completely on one's relation to the temporally conditioned constructs of language itself. Thus, there appears to be an ideological moment in which the specular memory of wholeness becomes misconstrued as a figural totality, deflecting the quest for identity into one of several authorizing discourses and narrative strategies. Rilke's fragmented narrative might therefore be regarded as a refusal to become implicated in this ideological transaction, a move which contains its own tacit ideological or even anti-ideological dimensions.

There are two significant moments in the movement of Rilke's text that help us to visualize the conception of subjectivity to which Malte aspires. Malte's depiction of the ruins of the Roman amphitheater at Orange corresponds to Lacan's own description of the intersubjective and reactive nature of the formation of the "I" as "symbolized in dreams by a fortress, or a stadium—its inner arena and enclosure, surrounded by marshes and rubbish-tips" (*Ecrits* 5). Indeed, from the beginning, we have the feeling that Malte's description has little to do with a tourist's account of an ancient ruin. Once inside, surrounded by "marsh-mallow shrubs" and the "prone columns," he initially fails to recognize the outlines of the theater itself. Malte's gaze falls first on the "open shell of the auditorium with its ascending tiers of seats" (217), on which, higher up, a few curious strangers are standing. At first, he tells us that these strangers, although a disturbing presence to him, are so small they are hardly worth mentioning. But his attention remains fixed on them because they appear to be looking at him—"they looked at me and wondered at my littleness" (217). Here again we witness the inversion that occurs so often in Malte's seeing, his intense consciousness of being seen by others. This self-constitution through the eyes of the Other is also what orients him toward the center of the theater—"that caused me to turn around" (217).

We might ask ourselves whether this turning around is also a turning inward, since the spectators appear to be looking at him and since what he sees, when he turns around, is not a literal event but a magnificent, invisible drama being enacted in the silence and emptiness of this vast and ancient space. "Ah, I was completely unprepared! A play was on. An immense, a superhuman drama was in progress, the drama of that gigantic scenery, the vertical tripartite structure of which was now visible, resonant in its immensity, overwhelming almost, and suddenly measurable by sheer excess of size" (217–18). What can Malte be referring to here but the intersubjective drama of the self? Not the self as some absolute essence by which each individual can be identified and distinguished from everyone else, but the self as an activity manifested in and through the theater of language. What was initially perceived only in fragments, then only from the point of view of the other, is suddenly grasped in its relational totality. In this sudden glimpse of the self as participant in a universal medium, Malte rediscovers his connection to humanity. In his attempt to express his individuality in language, he perceives the outlines of a common existence, discovering the materials of a self that he shares with all others and in whose construction we all participate.

> I yielded to a violent shock of pleasure. This which confronted me, with its shadows ordered in the semblance of a face, with the darkness concentrated in the mouth at the centre, bounded above by the symmetrically curled head-dress of the cornice: this was the mighty, all-disguising, antique mask, behind which the universe condensed into a face. Here in this vast amphitheatre of seats, there reigned a waiting, empty, absorbent existence: all happening was yonder, gods and destiny; and thence (when one looked up high) came lightly, over the groining of the wall, the eternal procession of the heavens. (218)

The body or the face may provide an initial imago of the self as a totality, but once we have "come outside of ourselves," to use Hegel's phrase, a more protective image for the "socialized I" must be found. If the ego is seen as a Roman stadium, it is because there is a contest going on in its inner arena. If the ego is seen as a fortress, it is because it requires a protective enclosure to keep out the forces it perceives as threatening to destroy it. The theater embodies both these aspects: it represents both the hermetic enclosure and the intersubjective space in which we constitute ourselves as actors for the world. Within this protective circle the self is determined by and plays to its otherness. But behind this image of the socialized I, Malte also recognizes the primordial image of the human face, not as an origin, but as a cultural representation of a lost origin, the verbal mask behind which the community of human faces can be condensed. This is the image of unity for which Malte is striving. The mask in which he initially loses himself, the strange and suffocating bourgeois mask of his Grandfather Brahe, or the various other faces he tries on and rejects, must be exchanged for a "more valid, more permanent" mask in which he can again find his way back to community.

Malte's discovery of the universal amphitheater of the self explains why he is so critical of the theater of his own day, and why he complains so bitterly about the "third party" introduced into drama in late classical antiquity and which so dominates the theater of his own time. According to Malte, this complication of the classical dramatic confrontation only obfuscates the essential drama within. For Malte, modern drama perpetually avoids this internal reality, to the extent that we have even lost the common language by which such a reality can be expressed. The implications of this critique extend far beyond our bounded conception of the function of aesthetic production. Theater in its authentic state belonged to religious experience; this is the state to which Malte would see it return. As if in afterthought, he establishes this connection in the margin of his text, realizing perhaps that he should not take for granted what he considers as the crucial link between authentic drama and God. "Let us be honest about it, then; we do not possess a theatre, any more than we possess a God: for this, community is needed. Every man has his own particular ideas and fears, and he allows others to see as much of them as is useful for him and as suits him. We continually spin out our faculty of understanding, that it may suffice us, instead of crying out to the icon-wall of our common misery, behind which the Inscrutable would have time to gather itself, and put forth all its strength" (218–19).

If Malte chooses the theater and the mask of classical antiquity as the specular model of the socialized I, the drama he singles out to represent the narrative of individual identity is none other than that of Oedipus, that is to say, Freud's Oedipus. The association of the oedipal model with a specular order is most clearly depicted in the diary entry that concludes part 1 of the *Notebook*, Malte's interpretation of the famous late fifteenth century tapestries known as *La Dame à la Licorne.*

Initially Malte describes a group of young women sketching these tapestries at the Museum of Cluny in Paris. For Malte, the very activity of sketching has become an alternative to the traditional notion of religious salvation based on Christ's familial model. "The path has somehow become narrower: families can no longer approach God. So there remained only certain other things that might at need be shared. But then, if the division was fairly made, so shamefully little came to each person; and if deception were practised in it, disputes arose. No, it is really better to sketch, no matter what. In time some resemblance will appear; and Art, especially when one acquires it thus gradually, is after all a truly enviable possession" (127). Nevertheless, unable to identify fully with the young women sketching the tapestries, Malte criticizes these would-be artists for failing to recognize the deeper ontological function of their sketching activities. "And in their intense absorption with the task they have undertaken, these young women, they never lift their eyes. They do not perceive that with all their strenuous copying they do nothing save to suppress within themselves the unalterable life opened before them, radiant and endlessly ineffable, in these woven pictures" (127). In direct contrast to the idea of sketching as reproduction, Malte's own interpretation must be understood in the original sense of the Greek *hermeneuein* — "to lay open," an exposure of what is hidden in the interpreter's own nature. Max Ernst once said: "Just as the role of the poet . . . consists in writing under the dictation of what is being thought, of what articulates itself in him, the role of the painter is to grasp and project what is seen in him" (Merleau Ponty 167). For Malte these operations become inextricably linked to one another; in his tapestry interpretations we see a fusion of both, a thinking seeing, a re-membering of fragments whose connections open up the mystery of his own being.

Originally intended to represent the five senses and with the addition of a sixth sense of love or desire, which may have originated with a separate group of hangings, the tapestries are completely rearranged in Malte's narrative. Instead of the traditional arrangement of sight, hearing, smell, touch, taste, and ending with the tapestry entitled "to my sole desire," Malte's interpretation begins with the sense of taste, followed by smell, hearing, "to my sole desire," touch, and finally sight (Small 39). The significance of this rearrangement may be better appreciated if we make passing reference to one of Rilke's later prose works entitled "Ur-Geräusch" (*Gesammelte Werke* 285–94). In this short essay Rilke continues the line of thought begun in Malte's tapestry interpretations by propounding an aesthetic which links perception to an ideal state of loving, the very ideal of passion that Malte celebrates in his *Notebook*. Rilke begins his argument with the complaint that Western poetry tends to emphasize the sense of sight over the other senses. Ideally, poetry should record the combined impression of the senses (or at least treat them with formal equality, as in certain Arabic poems). But if, as he argues, such a poetic synesthesia is analogous to the experience of loving, there are crucial differences between the two situations. Although, according to Rilke, those who love and those who create stand at the very center of the incoming streams of the senses, the former are so overwhelmed by their experience that they are unable to distinguish its various details. Artists, by contrast, are sufficiently immune to this inundation through the senses to focus on the particularities of their experience, making use of them in order to leap "through all five gardens [of the senses] at once" (293). The danger facing the lover is the unexpansiveness and hence helplessness of the lover's position. The danger to poets lies in the risks entailed when they explore the border lines which separate one order of their senses from another, testing the very limits of their experience.

Rilke's interpretation of the tapestries is precisely an attempt to leap through the gardens of the senses at once. By so doing, he annuls the original intent of the weavings as static and separate representations of the human senses in favor of a narrative of development culminating in the combined sensibility of the poetic spirit. Each of these tapestries depicts what he sees as the same island but at a different moment in its history. "There is always that oval, blue island, floating on a background of modest red, which is decked with flowers and inhabited by tiny animals busy with their own affairs. Only yonder, in the last hanging, the island rises a little, as if it had grown lighter" (119). The fact that Malte has changed the order of the hangings by shifting the "higher" island of sight from first to last place already suggests some kind of developmental sequence, the key to which must be sought in Malte's interpretations or, as several standard works on Rilke attest, in the biography of Rilke himself.

More than one critic has remarked on Rilke's predilection for islands. H. F. Peters points out that the island was a symbol of isolation for Rilke, a "piece of land cut off from the main" (39). Erich Simenauer gives us a more psychoanalytically attuned interpretation when he indicates that island images, in general, symbolize protection and security and that, in Rilke's work, they are identified with a "womb fantasy" (299). In this sense, we might link Malte's island interpretations to developments in Malte's relationship to his mother. A number of factors reinforce this tie. The only other time that we are told about Malte's predilection for islands is in reference to his childhood drawings, and then it is his mother who insists that the drawings represent islands, regardless of his intentions. The mother's assurance in this matter indicates the degree to which she sees herself as central in her son's landscape, and the fact that Malte recognizes the central figure on all the islands as the same person suggests his own confirmation of this attachment. "It has always one figure on it, a lady, in various costumes, but she is always the same" (120). Later, Malte leaves no doubt about this identification when he associates the color and material of his mother's dress with a gown worn by the Dame à la Licorne at a crucial phase in the developmental sequence.

We might also take into account that Malte's interpretation of the tapestries is addressed to Abelone, the only person ever specifically addressed in the novel—Abelone, Malte's mother's "youngest sister" (83), to whom Malte transfers his love after his return from boarding school, and with whom Malte has his first sexual experiences. I would not be the first to remark, moreover, on the resemblance of the name and character of Abelone to that of Lou Andreas-Salomé, who became something of a mother figure to Rilke. Indeed, as I mentioned earlier, Rilke's friend, lover, and lifelong confidant seems to be connected to the novel in several ways. In Rilke's early letters to Salomé we discover that he had from the beginning felt compelled to write a journal of his inner life to her but, in his initial attempt, had realized that he did not yet have the maturity as a writer. In one letter he even anticipates the island imagery of the tapestry interpretations when he describes some particularly pleasurable hour they spent together: "Solche Stunden sind wie ein dicht umblühtes Inselland" (Such hours are like an island surrounded by dense foliage) (*Rilke-Salomé: Briefwechsel* 16).

Indeed, if Malte's tapestry interpretation brings to the surface those hidden aspects of his development in relation to the mother, it is a development which follows the progression articulated by

Jacques Lacan in his concepts of need, demand, and desire. On the first island the young woman is feeding a falcon. At her feet a small dog waits expectantly. A lion and a unicorn stand on either side, holding up banners. This picture of contentment can be understood as a representation of childhood, when individual identity is totally dependent on the fulfillment of needs. The sense of taste represents the first formative experience in the child's inner development. But in the expectant look of the young dog we may already see the emergence of a demand for love, which cannot be fulfilled on the basis of needs.

On the second island, the woman weaves a beautiful wreath of roses—a signal of emerging childhood sexuality. The sense of taste originally identified with need has given over to an association with smell, in effect separating it from its original attachment but at the same time preserving this attachment metonymically under the general auspice of demand. According to Lacan, "Demand annuls [*aufhebt*] the particularity of everything that can be granted by transmuting it into a proof of love. . . . It is necessary, that the particularity [of the need] thus abolished should reappear beyond demand" (*Ecrits* 286–87)—namely, in desire. This is further corroborated by the shift of animal symbols from the lion to the unicorn. The lion is described by his loss of role as standard-bearer ("The lion no longer takes part"), but the tie between the woman and the unicorn becomes apparent ("but the unicorn on the right understands," 120). What the unicorn understands is not altogether clear, but one is inclined to think that it has to do with the woman's garland of roses, which may very well be used to wreath the unicorn. We further see the sublimation of an initial childhood sexuality in the image of the unused basket of roses which a monkey has uncovered, but which are transformed into carnations.

In the third tapestry, representing hearing, the overall tone of the scene is more subdued. The young woman, now playing an organ, is described as more beautiful than ever. Her beauty is also shared by the unicorn, who looks as if he is flowing in an "undulating motion" (*wie in Wellen bewegt*). The lion, by contrast, is out of sorts and dislikes the music played on the organ. A servant girl now accompanies the maiden and assists her at the organ by operating the bellows. Such a doubling may be understood as a sublimation in which the initial attachment to the mother is transferred onto a second person, a younger sister, Abelone, in order to avoid the repercussions of guilt. This conjecture is reinforced by the scene in the following tapestry.

The next island has grown larger, as if some kind of development has taken place. A tent has been set up. The maiden almost seems "homely" (*schlicht*) in her queenly attire. The servant girl who appeared in the previous tapestry has opened a small casket from which she lifts a precious ornament—"she lifts from it a chain, a ponderous, magnificent ornament that has always been kept under lock and key" (121). The object of desire, which was earlier linked to the childhood attachment to the mother, has now been transformed into a generalized object of veneration and no longer belongs solely to the central figure. It is an object secured by a chain which is at once the wreath of roses but also the device by which the wearer is secured to his desires. The little expectant dog that we saw in the first tapestry has reappeared, but now he is in a position of prominence: "The little dog sits beside her on a high place prepared for it, and looks on" (121). Since the German phrase *sieht es an* conveys the more specific sense of looking "at it," the woman seems to be taking the precious ornament out of the casket solely for the sake of showing this little dog. Fittingly, Malte points out that the motto of the tapestry is "A mon seul desir" (121).

The fifth island seems to portray suspense and danger, but its description is couched in such ambiguous terms that it reminds me of Freud's references to the antithetical sense of primal words in dreams and in primitive languages ("Antithetical Meaning" 155–61). A rabbit is running or fleeing in one corner. The woman is either holding up or supporting herself by a banner. With the other hand she grasps the horn of the unicorn. Malte asks himself whether something tragic has occurred: "Is this mourning? Can mourning stand so straight? And can a mourning-garment be so mute as that green-black velvet with its lustreless folds?" (121–22). I suspect that the answer to the question may be both yes and no. It is a mourning in the sense that the inevitable has happened—the young woman has finally touched the unicorn—and that this inevitability represents some sort of danger, perhaps from the outside. But it is also a moment of victory, as we see on the next and final tapestry, the one in which the island is higher than the rest. Here we see the meaning of the development in its positive light: there is a festival, one to which no one is invited. The lion has finally discovered his role as a guardian who holds everything at bay: "The lion looks around almost threateningly: no one may come" (122). And in this protected enclosure, the unicorn is able to fulfill his purpose undisturbed: "and the flattered animal bridles and rears and leans against her lap" (122). With the unicorn's head against her lap, and the young woman showing him a reflection of himself in a mirror, we cannot doubt that the image that he sees in this mirror is one of narcissistic fulfillment. Malte's last appeal is to Abelone: "Abelone, I imagine [*bilde mir ein*] that you are here. Do you understand, Abelone? I think you must understand" (122). This appeal completes the story of Malte's *Einbildung*—that is, the projection of the development of his innermost identity to its moment of self-recognition.

Seen thus, the process can be interpreted as one of individuation whereby an initial attachment, formed without one's own initiative, has become impossible and is restructured in such a way that it again becomes possible—and by itself. This imaginary identification is projected again and again onto subsequent relations in Malte's adulthood. Indeed, in the narrative which Malte's "sketching" activity creates out of the tapestries at Cluny, we can perceive the outlines of what psychoanalysis would consider a failure to resolve the Oedipus complex, since the island's final elevation and integrity appear to have been achieved without the legitimizing presence of the father.

If the resolution of the Oedipus complex involves the dissolution of the child's attachment to the mother through the father's interdiction, the tapestry interpretation seems to depict an oedipal conclusion, in which the mother remains at the center of Malte's adult identity. The persistence of this intimate mother/child attachment and the ways in which the father's threat is surmounted can be traced through several of Malte's childhood reminiscences. Remembering how once, while in a fever, he cried until his parents were summoned from the crown prince's ball, Malte describes how his father's interruption put an end to a tearful reunion between his mother and himself. But this initial interdiction does not imply an immediate dissolution of the Oedipus complex. After his parents return to the ball, Malte clings to his mother's dance program and lays her camellias on his eyes to preserve the new feelings generated by her "enchanting" presence. From that moment on, there is an attempt on both their parts to prolong their mutual attachment without incurring a new prohibition. We are told that their regular evening hour spent together acquires a measure of pretense. They read books, not because they are genuinely interested in them, but because they want to seem occupied in case the father appears.

Moreover, it is not merely toward the real father that this charade must be carried out. Malte also begins to pretend that he is his mother's little girl, Sophie. And when in later reminiscences his mother suggests to him that Sophie must certainly be dead, he "stubbornly . . . contradict[s] her and implore[s] her not to believe that, however little proof there might be to the contrary" (93–94). Indeed, Malte's continued identification with girls and young women gives us good reason to believe that Sophie is still very much alive, that the oedipal relation has not been resolved but has undergone a series of imaginary vicissitudes in order to preserve the original emotional attachment.

At one crucial stage in his fantasies we find an identification between young girls "in the neighborhood" and an elderly man, a scholar, an authority in Greek texts and a translator of certain obscure fragments of Sappho's poetry. This "solitary thinker" finds himself attracted to one of these girls in particular, not for his own sake, we are told, but for hers. She, in turn, is attracted to his love of learning, his wisdom. We might even speculate that this special girl might be the "lost" Sophie, since the name signifies a love of wisdom for its own sake. If Malte's previous masquerade as Sophie was an attempt to remain near the mother, in this new identification he appears to transform the figure of the mother into a man and to project himself into a platonic relation with this older male as a young woman. But underneath there appears to be a homosexual aspect refusing to be recognized as such. This disguised or circumvented homosexuality is further complicated by the fact that the scholar resolves to tell the young girl not of his own concern for her but of the lesbian poet Sappho, in effect, taking on the mask of a woman. It would seem, then, that the childhood relation to the mother is finally reestablished, but as a lesbian relationship. But the masquerade does not end here. Sappho, we are told, celebrates a "homoerotic" passion intended to prepare her young lover for heterosexual marriage, but the passion has "overreached" its intended object, surpassing even the "splendour" of a god.

In this complex fantasy we discover Malte's link between eros and agape, as an unfulfilled, "impossible" desire undergoes a series of transfigurations only to find its way to religious hope. But in order to reach this stage the fantasy must fulfill three separate emotional aims: it must alleviate an intolerable anxiety in the face of heterosexual union, it must reinstate the childhood relation to the mother without incurring the prohibition that this relation implies, and it must offer a way out of a homosexual object choice. And yet, according to Freud, where the Oedipus complex has not been entirely resolved, there is still the question of the missing phallus. For if the primary image of the self as a totality is the body, we must assume that certain anatomical differences cannot be suppressed but must be dealt with in one way or another. Certainly, Malte's overwhelming need to return to his childhood as if to solve some pressing dilemma attests to this assumption.

Toward the end of his journal Malte alludes to a small jewel case which he once found as a child:

> I still remember exactly how, one day long ago, at home, I found a jewel-casket. It was two hands-breadths large, fan-shaped, with an inlaid border of flowers on dark-green Morocco velvet, I opened it: it was empty. I can only say this now after so many years. But at the time when I had opened it I saw only in what its emptiness consisted: in velvet, a little mound of light-coloured velvet, no longer fresh; in the groove where the jewel had lain, which, empty now but lighter by a trace of melancholy, disappeared into it. For an instant might this be endured. But with those who are backward in loving it is perhaps always thus. (222)

The description recalls the former "jewel casket" which Malte describes in his tapestry interpretation at the Museum of Cluny, only there are crucial differences between the real and the imaginary casket. As described in detail earlier, the tapestry depicts a young maiden opening a small box and lifting from it "a chain, a ponderous, magnificent ornament that has always been kept under lock and key" (121). Beside her a small expectant dog sits in a place which has been prepared for him, and the object in her hand seems to be there for his sake alone. When we turn our attention to the real casket scene, Malte describes a similar container, only now he goes into far greater detail. It is described as "fan-shaped," "two hands-breadths wide," and bordered by a floral inscription. When opened, this mysterious container reveals a dark-green Morocco velvet, the same color and material of the dress of the Dame à la Licorne. Moreover, in the place where the "precious ornament" should have been, he sees only the groove, the emptiness in which this groove consists, running across the "little mound of light-coloured velvet." It seems almost superfluous to add that the German word for jewelry casket—*Schmucketui*—bears the unmistakable colloquial connotation of the female genitalia. Malte returns to the scene of the casket only to admit that it was empty. For it must certainly be an admission if he can only "say this after so many years." At the time Malte could endure the emptiness of the casket for only an instant, and then he had to find a way to overcome its awful implications.

"Wo es war soll ich werden!" Freud points to the psychological necessity of such returns with brilliant concision. Indeed, Malte's interpretations and reminiscences, like the progress of an analysis itself, tend to move ever closer to that primal scene which he attributes to the opening of the jewelry casket. The prolongation of his oedipal attachment through his identifications with girls and his attachment to the mysterious Abelone may have given him more time, but it does not solve the dilemma brought about by the missing ornament. The problem remains—"es war nicht da!" In other words, it was not there where he thought it was, and in order to rectify the matter, he had to put himself in its place, or, as Lacan puts it, "become the phallus for the mother" (*Ecrits* 281). We can speculate that it is through the writing of his journal that Malte makes this offering to the mother—not the real mother, however, but a real or figurative mother substitute, the reader as mother, the "Abelone" both inside and outside of the text.

Freud tells us that an improper mastery of the Oedipus complex means that the whole process of ego/superego formation must begin again at some later stage, causing the drama of childhood to be played out on an entirely new level. Since Malte's oedipal attachments were not immediately resolved by "rapid sublimation and identification [with the father]," his solution must be sought at all levels of adult aspiration—not only in his sexual identifications, but also in his political affiliations, religious sentiments, and artistic endeavors.

At the level of religious aspiration we know that Rilke did not find the answer in Christianity. This rejection of Christianity has the same source as Rilke's mistrust of psychoanalysis. Provisionally, we might link this rejection to what Freud calls a "renunciation of the father" as in his explanation of the "homosexual" source of Leonardo da Vinci's genius ("Leonardo da Vinci"). But unlike da Vinci's solution, which results in a compulsive curiosity about "mother nature," Rilke's situation represents an endless preoccupation with internal tensions which he must bring to light and resolve through his art. Rilke's refusal to designate a symbol of closure may appear to be a departure from the oedipal paradigm, but it is not a rejection of the father. It is merely a deferral, a suspension of the ultimate designation in favor of an unconditional justification of the subject: "He [the prodigal] was now terribly difficult to love, and he felt that One alone was capable of loving him. But He was not yet willing" (243).

In *Moses and Monotheism*, Freud argues that Christianity constituted a psychological innovation over Judaism because it shifted the emphasis of authority from the harsh oedipal phantasm to the son's designation of a loving, benevolent father, in effect conferring more individual freedom and responsibility onto the son in the generational transfer of authority (7–137). In the first place, it reaffirmed through its story of the crucifixion the psychological primacy of the guilt for the murder of the primal father. Paul, Freud argues, was the first to recognize the psychological power of this deep-seated guilt, which he called original sin. But he also recognized the importance of atonement and saw in Christianity the magnificent logic of sacrificing Christ, who, as Freud says, represents both the ringleader of the primal conspiracy and the innocent victim of the deep fear of retribution from the father. Paul's conversion, he argues, shifted the paradigm from a religion of the Father to a religion of the Son. But as the difference between Malte's and Jesus' parable of the prodigal son makes clear, it is a shift in focus, not in essence. Christ may have been sacrificed to atone for the primal murder, but he is also raised to the level of father-substitute. Thus, what is perceived to be a religion of the Son turns out to be a disguised tribute to the Father.

Although Malte recognizes the psychological power of Christianity, he rejects its solution as a compromise: "I believe that only Jesus could bear them, who still has resurrection in all His limbs: but they matter little to Him. It is only those who love that draw Him to them; not those who wait with a small talent for being loved, as with a lamp gone cold" (*Notebook* 201). According to Malte, Christ's sacrifice does not save those fragmented souls, "backward in loving" like himself, whose inner orientations make them "terribly difficult to love." Thus, if Malte "goes under," it is possibly because Rilke wanted him to be a radically new kind of savior, an "other" savior fashioned in language and brought to a deeply personal Golgotha in order to save himself. What Rilke discovered, however, was that by leaving the space for the father open, a once-and-for-all salvation became impossible. The alternative was a continual projection from the depths of the suffering self borne of a desire to repossess the security and contentment established in the earliest relationship with the parents.

Perhaps this is the critical point at which a separation occurs in the shared trajectory between Rilke's own articles of faith and those of psychoanalysis and Christianity, a point at which the gravitational field of social concern exerts its strongest influence over these attainments. For it is here that the problematic image of the father finds its resolution in a symbol linking individual desire with social authority—in the ego ideal, or in Christ, or even, as Paul Ricoeur argues, in the penates of Western law ("Fatherhood" 468–97). According to Rilke's conception, in contrast, art does not necessarily obey this law of gravity and therefore projects its imaginary vector out beyond the attainments of other socially responsible discourses. As Freud was to admit much later when once again dealing with the problematic image of the father, "Before the problem of the creative artist analysis must, alas, lay down its arms" ("Dostoevsky and Parricide" 177).

For all that, art can never resolve the question of salvation; it can only establish a direction and declare everything unfinished. By opening up to us the "more spacious world of pain," the poet offers us glimpses of what has not yet been gathered up by the "economies" of hope, justice, and desire. It is a moment of human possibility we can share only temporarily, before we return to our more comfortable, repressive gods and to our self-righteous equation, "culture equals resolution of conflict." But may we not at least entertain the suspicion that Rilke, who is at once the author and reader of his "other self," the patient and analyst, the confessant and the priest, has shown us a deeper vision of culture, the longer, harder, but ultimately more rewarding labor of the self on its own impossible path to salvation? Might we not speculate that true cultural attainment is dialectical, that it always also involves a refusal to reinstate the father, and that the dissolution of the Oedipus complex is only the holding pattern, the way in which cultures retain their authoritative norms, but also grow brittle and self-destructive?

III

From Elder Son to Big Brother: The Death of the Freudian Subject in Orwell's *Nineteen Eighty-Four*

CHAPTER 9

The Vicissitudes of an "Instinct" in the Conversion of Paul

If Malte Brigge's version of the prodigal son story distinguishes itself from the traditional parable of salvation because of the "abolition" of the father, it also does so because it conspicuously leaves out the part played by the elder son. Jesus' parable tells the story of two sons—the prodigal and his elder brother. The latter remains at home, working in his father's fields, remaining faithful to his father's commands. Unlike Rilke's legend, the original parable assumes that authority can be obtained only through the father. What becomes emphasized at the end of the parable is the brothers' competition and the older brother's seemingly valid complaint that he has been treated unfairly:

> Now the elder son was out in the fields, and on his way back, as he drew near the house, he could hear music and dancing. Calling to one of the servants, he asked what it was about. "Your brother has come," replied the servant, "and your father has killed the calf we had fattened because he has got him back safe and sound." He was angry then and refused to go in, and his father came out to plead with him; but he answered his father, "Look, all these years I have slaved for you and never once disobeyed your orders, yet you never offered me so much as a kid to celebrate with my friends. But, for this son of yours, when he comes back after swallowing up all your property—he and his women—you kill the calf we had been fattening." (Luke 15:25–30)

Jesus' parable sets forth more than a paradigm for human salvation; within its framework of departure and return, we are introduced to the problem of reconciling fatherly love between brothers. By stressing that the return represents a viable alternative to authority, the parable emphasizes the socially disruptive element of the Christian message. It upholds a radically new way of obtaining authority without having to submit to the traditional models of seniority in the Judaic family tradition. Thus, the parable of the prodigal son establishes a polarity between the older and the younger brother in the very way in which they seek favor from the father, a polarity which can also be seen in the distinctly different personalities which Paul exhibits before and after his conversion.

As the prototype of Christian conversion, Paul's turning to Christianity is essentially an expression of the younger son's bid for authority. But it is more than that. The transformation of identity from Saul to Paul also expresses the transference of authority from the elder brother to the younger son. Saul, the favored son of the Pharisaic sect, represents the unswerving acceptance of the father. He fulfills his obligations, obeys the laws, essentially trying to be an extension of his sect's authoritative identity. The converted Paul, by contrast, represents that new approach to authority which entails an initial rejection of the father, a harsh tutelage in the world, a return at the risk of rejection, and a triumphal reacceptance in spite of that risk.

If Paul's conversion reenacts the transference of authority from the elder son to the wayward younger brother, we can see by the ending of Jesus' parable that it is a transference which does not go unchallenged by the older brother. We can speculate that the father's response to his oldest son's complaint is of little comfort: "My son, you are with me always and all I have is yours. But it was only right we should celebrate and rejoice, because your brother here was dead and has come back to life; he was lost and is found" (Luke 15:31–32). Rather than resolving the situation, the father's acceptance of the prodigal creates the conditions for a brotherly struggle for power which will go on indefinitely, or at least until one or the other brother is mastered or killed.

Paul's conversion on the road to Damascus expresses the transference of authority within this brotherly struggle for mastery in its most radical form. It depicts a complete inversion of attitude and belief, a change from one way of life into its opposite—in short, an enantiodromia. As a member of the Pharisaic sect, Paul's aim is to suppress actively the Christian threat to his Judaic tradition. As a converted Christian, his aim is to find his way back to the father by loving his enemies in spite of their persecution. Both aims, although completely opposite in content, are alternative means to the same father, and as such they involve some form of renunciation or repression.

We might call Saul's active form of repression a *political* means to authority, and Paul's passive form of self-mastery a *religious* means. As pure concepts, these two orientations arise out of our need for control and our need for freedom. That the desire for power or mastery lies at the root of politics is obvious. Political power is by definition concerned with control or domination of others. It achieves this goal by direct, sensible persuasion. Religion, in contrast, arises out of the conviction that we are not in control of our fate. Hence its primary goal is not power per se but freedom. It achieves this goal by indirect means, appealing to belief and conscience rather than knowledge and sensibility. Inasmuch as we are never completely free from oppression or completely in control of our fate, religious and political desire are inseparably linked, constantly vying for a dominant position in our minds. Conversion in one direction or the other is purely a tendency to adopt an ideology which addresses our prevailing needs and a commitment to follow absolutely this newly won conception of life. The struggle between brothers vying for fatherly love thus suggests a constant tension between religious and political authority, each sharpening its powers of self-determination against the other. This opposition implies an endless refinement in the realms both of political power and of religious self-mastery, and it is this implication which the following chapters seek to explore.

It is no coincidence that the type of conversion represented by Paul is also an essential ingredient of modern political ideology. Like many Christians, political ideologists divide the world into good and evil, the elect and the damned, and try to solicit as many members into the former categories as possible. The best-known literary example of a modern political conversion can be found in George Orwell's *Nineteen Eighty-Four.* Indeed, if the conversion of Paul represents the privileging of the religion of the younger son, the conversion of Winston Smith to party totalitarianism represents the political alternative which we can readily recognize as the religion of Big Brother. In structure, both conversions are alike, exemplifying complete inversions of attitude and belief. Both present the individual's total acceptance of a stipulated set of beliefs which herald an era of social renewal. In content, however, Paul's and Winston's conversions are diametrically opposed to one another: Paul is transformed from an active adherent of the established politicoreligious order into a Christian dissident, but Winston Smith is converted from rebellion against the status quo to passive conformity with it. Furthermore, when we consider the conversion of Paul as the death of the old individual and the birth of a new one, we can also recognize in this polarity the relation between the figures of Winston Smith and his persecutor, O'Brien. In many ways the unconverted Saul is very much like O'Brien. Both men belong to the strict inner parties of their respective political organizations. Saul is a member of the Pharisees, one of the most orthodox Hebrew sects; O'Brien is a privileged member of the inner party of Ingsoc. Both men have similar duties. They seek out dissenters, persecute them, force them to recant, and, if their respective organizations so desire, have them killed. But the parallel ends most abruptly. Paul suddenly and enigmatically turns his life around, while O'Brien continues in his role as inquisitor. This leaves us with several initial questions. What makes Paul change into the opposite of what he was? What special powers does O'Brien have that make him invulnerable to this change? Why does Winston Smith have to undergo a "conversion" instead of O'Brien?

With regard to the first question, I have limited the discussion to one primary text—Acts 26:4–18, the most famous and influential story of Paul's conversion. The story is not autobiographical in any of the senses we have met with before; it does not even belong to the Pauline canon. But as a representation of Paul's conversion, it has become embedded in Christian consciousness, in essence, becoming the mythical representation of an event whose meaning lies not in its historical significance but in its figural impact on subsequent Christian aspirations. The name "Paul" is a literary designation which refers primarily to those authorized texts in the Bible in which he appears, either as a writer or as a character. "Paul" designates not only the rebirth of a historical figure but the incarnation of a more permanent, public self no longer identifiable with the historical personage submerged by the process of writing. Like the body markings of the primitive tribesman, the name becomes metonymous for a particular body of texts which together make up the identifying inscriptions of a new, social self created in and by language.

To what may we attribute Paul's enantiodromia? If in Paul's case this is a question of interiority, the answer may be difficult to infer only from the text itself. Before becoming a Christian, Paul is known as a zealous follower of the Pharisaic law. In response to a growing threat from Christianity, he obtains a commission from the high priests in Jerusalem to seek out and arrest members of the new religious movement and bring them back to Jerusalem for trial. This is not merely a dispassionate duty he performs in the service of higher authority. Rather, as he himself concedes to King Agrippa, it is an act of personal vindication: "I myself thought it my duty to work actively against the name of Jesus of Nazareth" (Acts 26:9). Saul receives his authority from the chief priests because he asks for it. And when Christians are sentenced to death as a result of his endeavors, he votes his enthusiastic assent. His vindictiveness toward the followers of Christ borders on the obsessional: "In all the synagogues I tried by repeated punishment to make them renounce their faith; indeed my fury rose to such a pitch that I extended my persecution to foreign cities" (Acts 26:11). In view of this obsessive, vindictive nature, Paul's sudden and complete transformation to Christian humility and love of his enemy is startling, to say the least. But if we pursue Paul's obsession with persecution in the light of a further, more detailed psychological inquiry, enriching the content of the original story and giving it a universal significance, we are able to find at least a provisional explanation for the psychological motivation for his conversion.

In "Instincts and Their Vicissitudes" Freud describes two different ways in which an instinct may undergo modification: "reversal into its opposite" and "turning round upon the subject's own self" (128). Both of these forms of transformation seem to be central to Paul's conversion. In the case of enantiodromia, or "reversal into its opposite," Freud argues that there are two processes at work: "a change from activity into passivity, and a reversal of content" (127). To exemplify the first process he chooses two "minimal pairs" of drives—sadism/masochism, and scopophilia/exhibitionism—positing that each of the terms in these minimal pairs belong to the same instinct but that the aim of the instinct has changed. "The active aim (to torture, to look at) is replaced by the passive aim (to be tortured, to be looked at)" (127). The second process which Freud refers to as "reversal of content" can be found in the "single instance of the transformation of love into hate" (127). But, as Freud goes on to argue, if the reversal affects the aim of the instinct, changing it from active into passive, it must also entail a substitution of objects. Here Freud acknowledges that enantiodromia coincides with the category of "turning round upon the subject's own self." "The turning round of an instinct upon the subject's own self is made plausible by the reflection that masochism is actually sadism turned round upon the subject's own ego, and the exhibitionism includes looking at his own body. Analytic observation, indeed, leaves us no doubt that the masochist shares in the enjoyment of the assault upon himself, and the exhibitionist shares in the enjoyment of [the sight of] his exposure" (127). At this point Freud is able to formulate the process by which sadism can turn into masochism:

> 1. Sadism consists in the exercise of violence or power upon some other person as object.
>
> 2. This object is given up and replaced by the subject's self. With the turning round upon the self, the change from an active to a passive instinctual aim is effected.
>
> 3. An extraneous person is once more sought as object; this person, in consequence of the alteration which has taken place in the instinctual aim, has to take over the role of the subject. (127)

Persecution, then, is an activity which for whatever reason preoccupies itself with its object. In Paul's case, the obsession with punishing Christians gives way to a deeply rooted identification with the objects of his persecution. His conversion to Christianity can then be seen as an internalization of the object of persecution, a process which is reflected in God's address to Paul: "Saul, Saul. Why do you persecute me? It hurts you to kick against the goads" (Acts 26:14). The message is that a person is somehow yoked to God like a dray animal to its cart and master. By persecuting Christians, Saul is kicking out against God the Father, thus only hurting himself.

Freud offers a tentative explanation as to why this transformation from sadism to masochism takes place in his observation that masochists take a degree of pleasure in pain: "For we have every reason to believe that sensations of pain, like other unpleasurable sensations, trench upon sexual excitation and produce a pleasurable condition, for the sake of which the subject will even willingly experience the unpleasure of pain" ("Instincts" 128). At this point, however, Freud does not go into detail as to how unpleasure "trenches" upon sexual excitation to produce a pleasurable condition. In fact, he categorically dismisses the idea that the original sadistic urge might itself be based on a prior stage of primal masochism in which the child cannot yet distinguish the sources of pain and pleasure and must therefore submit to them in a passive way. Only later does Freud reverse himself. By postulating this early stage of masochism, he is able to argue for a process which he calls "propping" whereby one system of aims leans on another system, thus establishing the possibility of associating unpleasurable feelings with the pleasurable experiences incurred during the infant stage (*Three Essays on the Theory of Sexuality* 203–4). What Paul might therefore have discovered on the road to Damascus is that he was caught in a "reflexive" or "middle" position in which he actually took pleasure in the experience of persecution—that by identifying with his victims, he was able to experience the pleasure of pain. From here it is a short step from reaction to affirmation, from oppression to acceptance. Once Paul is "blinded" by this insight, that is, once he turns his sight from the outward act to the inward experience of persecution, he can no longer remain on the middle ground but must proceed to Damascus to take up the superior pleasure of a Christian masochism.

But this "sexualized" interpretation of Paul's conversion seems somewhat limited. One might agree that infantile sexuality might well contribute to the process, but it cannot be the sole motivational factor. At this point we return to Freud's discussion of the other "minimal pair" of drives—scopophilia/exhibitionism—which, Freud argues, has an almost identical transformational pattern to that of sadism/masochism:

> 1. Looking as an *activity* directed toward an extraneous object.
>
> 2. Giving up of the object and turning of the scopophilic instinct towards a part of the subject's own body; with this, transformation to passivity and setting up of a new aim—that of being looked at.
>
> 3. Introduction of a new subject to whom one displays oneself in order to be looked at by him. ("Instincts" 129)

Unlike the case of sadism/masochism, however, here Freud postulates a phase which precedes active scopophilia which he calls auto-erotic. By this he means that the individual was originally preoccupied with a part of his or her own body, an interest which only later was exchanged for an analogous part of someone else's body. Freud does not tell us exactly how this exchange takes place, but we might infer that it has something to do with the child's discovery of sexual difference in others, which establishes the need to make comparisons for the sake of the child's own sexual identification.

Nevertheless, at this stage Freud does not make a crucial link between the transformations of sadism to masochism and scopophilia to exhibitionism. Instead of seeing these minimal pairs as inseparable aspects of a more fundamental process, each performing crucial functions for the other, he treats them as separate elements with separate causes. To make this link, we must turn to Lacan's conception of the mirror stage, in which the body image becomes the primordial image of the ego, and the discovery of the self is made possible only by the splitting of the primal childhood self into a dialectical relation between Subject and Other. What sadism/masochism and scopophilia/exhibitionism have in common is that they are both dominated by the generally informing laws of intersubjectivity. In order for a sadism/masochism inversion to take place, there must be a subject "looking at" and "being looked at" at the same time. The mirror stage explains how the desire to torture or to be tortured is a response to an internal relation between the subjective and the other self. The outward act becomes an objectification of one's identity in relation to the repressed. This identity can be formulated in one of two ways: either one identifies with the cause of the repression (the father), or one identifies with the repressed (the son). In the former case, one constitutes oneself from the perspective of the oppressed through sadism by mutilating the body image of the Other. In the latter case, one constitutes oneself from the perspective of the oppressor by turning the violence upon oneself.

In the case of Paul's conversion, we might say that he begins by identifying himself with the law of the father. He is able to achieve and sustain this identity, however, only by reenacting again and again the scene of the primal repression. But to sustain this identity as a persecutor, he must also constitute himself as a subject in the eyes of his victims. This leads to a dilemma. Inquisitors like Paul become so caught up in the thoughts and motives of their enemies that their identities become totally dependent on them. They discover that without an opposition to crush, or, more precisely, without an opposition to watch them exhibiting their strength, they have no power, no validity—they are incomplete. It is not difficult to see that by suppressing other people's ideas and beliefs, inquisitors are showing a certain respect for them, are in fact shaping their own identity in response to them, and when inquisitors realize that the act of suppression does not in itself give credence to their own values, the pathway to enantiodromia is made clear.

We might therefore infer that the process of enantiodromia occurs the moment Paul recognizes that the object he is persecuting is actually an externalized image of the self he is continually having to repress. He realizes that this "other self" is the real subject of his efforts and that his sadism is only a self-defeating attempt to reincorporate what he has lost. Rather than constituting himself by looking longingly at the punished subject, he wants to become that punished subject being looked at by others. For Paul, becoming a Christian means giving up the necessity of devoting all his energies against an externalized image of an internal scene which refuses to go away. Every Christian he persecutes is a reincarnation of what he has never been able totally to suppress within. Becoming a Christian therefore means constituting himself as a subject without continually having to affirm this identity through an expenditure of his own energy. Conversely stated, the masochism and exhibitionism of Paul's Christianity require less energy for the creation of identity than the scopophilia and sadism of Pharisaism.

CHAPTER 10

Inside the Writing Machine: The Diary of Winston Smith

It is important to note that the process of enantiodromia need not be an externalized phenomenon, performed "in the world"; writing itself offers an alternative occasion for externalizing the sadomasochistic, scopophilic-exhibitionistic urges. As I have pointed out earlier, the relationship of writers to language in general reflects their relation to the authority of the father. They may fully accept the unifying fabrications of the language into which they were born, or they may be intent on destroying them. They may use this language of authority to dominate their readers, or they may try to free themselves from it by struggling against its authoritativeness. Moreover, as writers and readers of their own life, they can re-create on a narrative plane what they experience on a specular plane. Writing becomes a temporal mirror by which they can perceive their own actions. It is no coincidence that Paul was a writer. Conversion of the kind that he undergoes depends on the ability to make oneself into a subject through one's writing, and to be able to sustain this image of the self through the production of permanent traces.

It is no surprise, then, that in *Nineteen Eighty-Four* Winston Smith's first act of retaliation against the totalitarian system entails the opening of a diary. The sheer act of writing in such a repressive system is considered treasonous: "He dipped his pen into the ink and then faltered for just a second. A tremor had gone through his bowels. To mark the paper was the decisive act" (11). Winston's job at the Ministry of Truth also involves writing, at least the rewriting or falsifying of past documentation. But it is significant that although Winston receives written directives from a pneumatic tube, he carries out their orders orally on his "speakwrite," after which he immediately disposes of the written instructions. Winston is one of hundreds of rewriters in the ministry, all connected through speakwrites (which signifies not only orality but orthodoxy) to a giant writing machine. This great writing apparatus "stands in" for all individual psychic writing machines by absolutely controlling all written traces. As a reflection of the human psyche, it performs the very same functions that the censor does in the ego in order to maintain the integrity of its own power structure. But by forbidding all recourse to the written trace, it annuls the possibility of externalizing and socializing individual memory, thus enabling it to perform its mediations for everyone. Any form of writing, any collection of written traces outside of its jurisdiction is considered intrinsically dangerous to the system and punishable by death. Books not within its control are rooted out and either burned or rewritten. The most dangerous book, purportedly written by the archenemy of Ingsoc, Emmanuel Goldstein, constantly eludes this fate, and it is fitting that this textbook of dissent has no other title but *The Book*, intimating the religious role that all written traces outside of Ingsoc's sphere of influence have. Winston's rebellion occurs when he attempts to constitute his own identity through the written word rather than to allow the party authority to shape him. At work, this means collecting shreds of evidence to convince himself of the monstrous lie upon which Ingsoc is based. At home, it means keeping a record of his innermost thoughts and through this introspection to try to sharpen his powers of self-determination against the authoritarian regime. Once he has set pen to paper, he is able to create a mirror of words for himself to substitute for the one offered by the emotionally charged propaganda and intentional misinformation of the telescreen.

In order to understand better the role of the diary form in *Nineteen Eighty-Four*, we should briefly recall the two other modern texts through which we have explored the idea of human salvation in twentieth-century autobiographical writing. Each of these texts introduces the diary form at a very different moment. In Joyce's *Portrait* this form emerges at the very end of the novel, implying that Stephen Dedalus's achievement of self-sufficiency coincides with the moment that writing becomes a medium for self-constitution. In Rilke's *Notebook*, we see the utilization of the diary form to break down the traditional narrative restrictions on self-consciousness. Rilke's revision of the parable of the prodigal son redefines the problem of human salvation and offers an alternative form of salvation in a demotic world. In *Nineteen Eighty-Four*, by contrast, we see the struggle and ultimate failure of the diary form to break through the authority of a traditional narrative structure. *Nineteen Eighty-Four* may be the story of a political capitulation, but it is first and foremost the story of a capitulation to language. Winston Smith's conversion can be seen as the failure of the diary writer to constitute himself through self-writing, and his subsequent capitulation to the totalizing narrative tradition of utopian "salvationist" fiction. Since Orwell's novel presents a struggle between the diary form and a plotted narrative, with the latter emerging as victor, it focuses on the personal loss and thus inverts the traditionally positive value assigned to utopian fiction. The dystopia is thus a novel of utopia which emphasizes individual loss over social gain, and in the case of *Nineteen Eighty-Four*, this involves the repression of a suitable means in language by which the writer is able to constitute himself.

The main reason why Winston Smith fails to constitute himself through self-writing is that he cannot project a satisfying audience for his writing. Writing has its own form of mirror stage. Just as children can form a unified conception of the self only through recognizing the totality of another body image, so writers can perceive themselves as a unity only by establishing a single, unified audience. Without being able to conceive of an audience, Winston is entirely at a loss as to what to write about:

> For whom, it suddenly occurred to him to wonder, was he writing this diary? For the future, for the unborn. His mind hovered for a moment round the doubtful date on the page, and then fetched up with a bump against the Newspeak word *doublethink*. For the first time the magnitude of the what he had undertaken came home to him. How could you communicate with the future? It was of its nature impossible. Either the future would resemble the present, in which case it would not listen to him, or it would be different from it, and his predicament would be meaningless. (12)

Winston's need to find an audience other than the one represented by Big Brother indicates his inability to identify with paternal authority in general, suggesting an inner conflict related to the oedipal phase. Richard Smyer argues that Winston's desire to keep a diary expresses a deeply felt need to understand the "primal crime" in which the original bond between mother and child was shattered by a violent and repressive authority: "The very act of setting pen to paper becomes the symbolic recreation of a fearful sexual adventure out of the personal, and mythic past, a past still alive in his soul. The earliest entries in his diary reveal traces of the primal crime and its consequence, the continuing tension between anarchic impulse and prohibition, in the new owner's mind" (144). Winston's first entry in the diary expresses his fixation with this primal scene in terms of external events. Writing in his own "childish handwriting," he describes a film in which a small boy clinging to a middle-aged woman "as though trying to burrow into her" is blown to pieces by an Oceanian bomb. Whether this scene is a "violent primal violation of the maternal figure," as Smyer suggests, or a violent dissolution of the oedipal attachment of the son to the mother, amounts to the same thing.

The psychological motivation for Winston's first diary entry seems to be corroborated by an altogether different set of associations which occur at the very moment of writing. "He did not know what had made him pour out this stream of rubbish. But the curious thing was that while he was doing so a totally different memory had clarified itself in his mind, to the point where he almost felt equal to writing it down. It was, he now realized, because of this incident that he suddenly decided to come home and begin the diary today" (13). The incident to which he refers has to do with two people who work in the Ministry of Truth: Julia, the girl from the fiction department, and O'Brien. Winston's attitude toward these two people projects the psychic consequences of that first scene of primal destruction. He finds himself hating Julia, as "he disliked nearly all women, and especially the young and pretty ones" (14). The reason for this hatred of women is the fact that his attraction for them is continually thwarted by the restrictions of the party. Moreover, it is women's complicity with these restrictions which angers him most: "It was always the women, and above all the young ones, who were the most bigoted adherents of the party" (14). Here we see an instance of the psychological process of reversal by which an initial feeling of love is transformed into hate. Because of the party's interdiction, that explosion of the mother's and child's bodies, frustrated attraction becomes transformed into a need to mutilate and destroy the body of the loved object. This is corroborated by Winston's conviction that he himself was guilty of the murder of his mother (142). But whether his violent urges are expressed as hatred toward women or guilt toward the mother, the real cause of his feelings is somewhere within Winston himself, something represented by his own body.

After suppressing the desire to smash Julia's skull with a cobblestone when he meets her by coincidence on the street, Winston suddenly realizes "that in moments of crisis one is never fighting against an external enemy but always against one's own body" (91). The desire to mutilate the other is thus combined with sexual desire, as if to fulfill the requirements to two antagonistic inner impulses: "Suddenly, by the sort of violent effort with which one wrenches one's head away from the pillow in a nightmare, Winston succeeded in transferring his hatred from the face on the screen to the dark-haired girl behind him. Vivid, beautiful hallucinations flashed through his mind. He would flog her to death with a rubber truncheon. He would tie her naked to a stake and shoot her full of arrows like Saint Sebastian. He would ravish her and cut her throat at the moment of climax" (18). The taboo placed on sexuality because of the violent repression that occurs when the Oedipus complex is destroyed causes Winston to identify with the repressive authority of the father. Sexual gratification can therefore be obtained only by channeling it through violence. Winston's sadistic tendency must therefore be linked to what he perceives as an original mutilation.

Since the dissolution of the Oedipus complex has to do with the discovery of sexual difference and its implications, we might conjecture that Winston's fixation on the mutilation of mother and child involves a deep-seated fear of castration. When the bomb explodes, killing the mother and child, Winston describes a camera shot of the child's severed arm flying through the air. It would not be difficult to surmise that the loss of the arm or hand might be related to the child's fear of losing his penis, since the loss of either could be directly related to the prohibition to masturbation. On a different occasion, just after a bomb explosion, Winston sees another severed hand, this time lying amid the rubble in his path. Covered with plaster, it looks to Winston like a plaster cast, and he takes the trouble to kick "the thing into the gutter" (76). The word "cast" also reminds us that Julia herself has her arm in a sling when she first meets Winston. He immediately conjectures that she may have crushed it in the "novel-writing machine," a sign perhaps of the consequences to one who masturbates.

Winston's uneasiness about sexual difference also returns in one of his next diary entries, in which he painfully records his sexual experience with a middle-aged prostitute. When he first meets her, her face is so thickly painted over with make-up that he mistakes her for a young girl. It is only afterward, when he is about to have intercourse with her, that he discovers her to be old, the same age as the woman with the boy in the film. His memory of the scene reenacts the horror of the childhood discovery: "She threw herself down on the bed, and at once, without any kind of preliminary, in the most coarse, horrible way you can imagine, pulled up her skirt. I— . . . I turned up the lamp. When I saw her in the light— . . . When I saw her in the light she was quite an old woman, fifty years old at least. But I went ahead and did it just the same" (63). What stands out in Winston's memory, however, is a realization so horrible that he cannot even commit it to paper, let alone pronounce by its proper name: "the truly dreadful detail was that her mouth had fallen a little open, revealing nothing except a cavernous blackness. She had no teeth at all" (63).

The shock of seeing a middle-aged woman with no teeth covers up and stands in for the much earlier shock of discovery that his mother lacks the organ which he has come to prize so highly. We may even surmise that Winston's irrational fear of rats is linked both to his castration anxiety and to the primordial shock of becoming detached from the mother's body. In their first rendezvous in the room above Mr. Charrington's shop, Julia chases away a rat by hurling a shoe at it "with a boyish jerk of her arm" (128). Winston's terror at the rat's presence is assuaged only after Julia completely envelopes him with her arms and legs, like the mother in the movie he formerly describes. What frightens Winston is not the physical danger that the rat represents but some inner peril which he has come to associate with rats:

> For several moments he had the feeling of being back in a nightmare which had recurred from time to time throughout his life. It was always very much the same. He was standing in front of a wall of darkness, and on the other side of it there was something unendurable, something too dreadful to be faced. In the dream his deepest feeling was always one of self-deception, because he did in fact know what was behind the wall of darkness. With a deadly effort, like wrenching a piece out of his own brain, he could even have dragged the thing into the open. He always woke up without discovering what it was, but somehow it was connected with what Julia had been saying when he cut her short. (128)

The almost conscious self-deception which Winston practices and which Julia is about to reveal, must be connected to the primal scene. Julia says, "Did you know they attack children? Yes, they do. In some of these streets a woman daren't leave a baby alone for two minutes. It's the great huge brown ones that do it. And the nasty thing is that the brutes always— " (128). We may be sure to complete the sentence just as Smyer does, by relating that nasty thing "to the infant's genital mutilation" (147). The image of the rat thus sheds light on the primal scene from two different perspectives. On the one hand, the rat leaving his hole in the wall projects the child's conviction that the penis somehow became detached from the mother and that she wants it back—reflecting his desire to become the phallus for the mother. On the other hand, the rat symbolizes the violence that castration anxiety conjures up in the child's imagination and is therefore also an image of the harsh paternal threat to the child's own body image. To become one with the mother and to be eaten by the father thus become condensed into one image. Significantly, the rat appears soon after Winston and Julia have gone to bed together. Julia is wearing make-up and the same perfume used by the aged prostitute whose toothless mouth had so horrified him earlier. The double bed reminds Winston of a bed that he occasionally slept in during his boyhood—his mother's bed. Only by cradling him like a baby in a protective, womblike embrace and by promising to "bung" up the hole with "plaster" is Julia able to quell Winston's childhood anxieties.

Winston's initial fear of and aggressivity toward women is counterbalanced by his identification with and attraction to O'Brien. Since Winston has no memory of his own father and refuses to identify himself with Big Brother, he is looking for an alternative father-figure, one who can both neutralize the violence of the primal act and be an understanding confessor who tolerates and forgives his feelings and desires. Winston's search for a paternal figure, which ends with his relation with O'Brien, is a necessary result of his determination to reject Big Brother: "He felt deeply drawn to him, and not solely because he was intrigued by the contrast between O'Brien's urbane manner and his prizefighter's physique. Much more it was because of a secretly held belief—or perhaps not even a belief, merely a hope—that O'Brien's political orthodoxy was not perfect. Something in his face suggested it irresistibly. And again, perhaps it was not even unorthodoxy that was written in his face, but simply intelligence" (14). Winston's identification with O'Brien is completely tied to his need to write himself down. Winston is looking for a reader who reflects the intelligence and openmindedness which he himself brings to bear in the reading of his own writing. The desire to project this receptivity onto another human face, however, also indicates how crucial it is for Winston to find an alternative authority which circumvents the authoritative presence of Big Brother. Only by anchoring his need for an authorizing presence in the human community, a "brotherhood" represented by a single human face, is Winston able to constitute a unified self in writing. As the rhetoric of the following line suggests, this self-constitution also means a reestablishment of masculine virility: "But no! His courage seemed suddenly to stiffen of its own accord. The face of O'Brien, not called up by any obvious association, had floated into his mind. He knew, with more certainty than before, that O'Brien was on his side. He was writing the diary for O'Brien—*to* O'Brien; it was like an interminable letter which no one would ever read, but which was addressed to a particular person and took its color from that fact" (73).

Once O'Brien has become Winston's projected father-confessor, Winston becomes freer to explore his inner world through the world around him. As he wanders about through the proletarian quarters of the city, he tries to find out more about those "prehistoric" times before the revolution. As Smyer argues, what Winston seems to be trying to recapture is that period of assurance in his own personal history, a golden time before the oedipal revolution when he experienced the unconditional love of his mother. Indeed, his purchase of the diary as well as his later purchase of a glass paperweight establish a relation between his quest for this "golden country" of childhood and writing. The diary is a "young lady's diary," and its creamy color "a little yellowed by age" (11) reminds him of the walls of his mother's bedroom. The paperweight, like a miniature protective womb, preserves a piece of coral, a fragile piece of formerly oceanic life. Both items hearken back to an earlier, more wholesome prehistoric time. Even the upstairs room in the junk shop in which Winston purchased these items awakens in Winston "a sort of nostalgia, a sort of ancestral memory" (86), and the bed in that room reminds him of his mother's bed. The experiences that follow Winston's initial act of writing are steeped in the coloration of early childhood, and like his effort to reconstruct the childish nursery rhyme, his desire to write is prompted by the need to reconstruct a shattered past in order to complete his fragmented identity.

Writing seems to have a neutralizing effect on Winston's terror and hatred of women. It is not surprising that the first sign of love that he receives from Julia comes in the form of a written note. But even more telling is the reversal of content of Winston's feelings for Julia the moment when she passes him the note. Only four days before, outside of Mr. Charrington's shop, Winston's encounter with Julia has prompted in him the desire to "smash her skull" (90) with the glass paperweight. Now in the brightly lit corridor of the Ministry of Truth, his attitude undergoes a change similar to the one described by Freud in the transformation from sadism to masochism. Seeing her with her arm in a sling does not give him any sadistic pleasure. Instead, he ponders the possible cause of her misfortune, speculating that she could have broken it in the "novel writing machine," which, as he muses, is a very common occurrence. And when Julia trips in front of him, falling directly on her injured arm, Winston suddenly identifies with her pain. "A curious emotion stirred in Winston's heart. In front of him was an enemy who was trying to kill him; in front of him, also, was a human creature, in pain and perhaps with a broken bone. Already he had instinctively started forward to help her. In the moment when he had seen her fall on the bandaged arm, it had been as though he felt the pain in his own body" (95). At this moment Winston discovers the truth of his statement about the innerness of his relations with the external world. During this flash of empathy, Winston is again able to make contact with the mother: "[Julia's] face had turned a milky yellow color" (95). He is again at the scene of the primal disaster, only this time he no longer identifies with the perpetrator of the crime, but with the victims of that original mutilation: the broken arm which he feels in another's body is the severed arm of the little boy which he wants to put back in its place. The need to reconstruct the human body—the primordial image of the ego—is reinforced by three simple words written on a scrap of paper and passed to him at the very moment when he reaches out to help another—"I love you."

CHAPTER II

Reforming Desire

FROM THE moment that Winston begins his surreptitious love affair with Julia, we lose sight of the diary. This disappearance has two very important implications. On the one hand, it signals the moment when Winston the writer becomes caught up in the novelistic plot that leads him to Room 101 in the Ministry of Love. On the other hand, this movement from writing to action becomes the means by which the process of self-discovery in writing becomes externalized, when the internal drama becomes enacted on a naturalistic stage. As we have seen, writing carries two different functions—one linked to desire, the other to authority. These different aims can be related to the two different kinds of instinctual forces posited by Freud: sexual instincts and ego instincts. The identification of the diary with both Julia and Winston's mother implies that the sexual relation to writing can be traced back to the oedipal phase. Writing on the creamy white paper is symbolic both of the sexual act and of the return to the womb. Not only is it a means, as Derrida says, by which one allows liquid to flow from a tube onto parchment, it is also a way of encasing an image of the self within its protective covers. But the desire to enclose an image of the unified self in the womblike security of a book presupposes the ability to authorize the fabrication of the unified self. This is where the autobiographical act must be linked to the establishment of authority, the identification with a fatherlike source which both mirrors the primordial body image and protects it from mutilation. If Winston's relation to Julia objectivizes the sexual instincts affiliated with writing, his relation to O'Brien objectivizes those ego instincts by which all threats to the self are continually repressed. As Freud has pointed out, the two kinds of instincts are interdependent but completely antagonistic.

It is important to note that Winston's "ego instincts," associated with O'Brien, are put into motion only after he has been able to liberate his sexual instincts. Once he can feel love for Julia, his initial sadistic and voyeuristic impulses undergo a reversal and are turned inward on his own ego. He is able to empathize with the pain of others as if it were happening in his own body. As a result of this turning inward, he has reached the "middle position" in which he is able to constitute himself as a subject through the gaze of the father. But the restoration of his sexual impulses requires the protection of a tolerant father, not a violent, castrating father represented by Big Brother. It is not enough to be protected by the comforting embrace of the mother. Alluding to the mother and child in the lifeboat on the ocean, Winston recalls his mother's inability to stave off her family's starvation: "When the last of the chocolate was gone, his mother had clasped the child in her arms. It was no use, it changed nothing, it did not produce more chocolate, it did not avert the child's death or her own. . . . The refugee woman in the boat had also covered the little boy with her arm, which was no more use against bullets than a sheet of paper" (146). Neither is writing on a sheet of paper enough; one can create a stabilized and secure self-image only by allying oneself with some form of authority and by undergoing the necessary modifications that such an authority demands. The fact that Winston and Julia go to see O'Brien together is therefore a crucial step. In order that the more primary sexual instincts are protected, they must find shelter within the ego's sanctifying enclosure. It is no coincidence that the walls in O'Brien's apartment are covered with cream-colored wallpaper or that the carpet is a rich, dark, "oceanic" blue; the inner sanctum of an Inner Party member is one step closer to the subdued, oceanic existence of the preoedipal phase. Neither is it a coincidence that when Winston and Julia undergo O'Brien's "catechismal" initiation into the Brotherhood, they agree to murder, cheat, mutilate children, and suffer torture—everything but be separated from each other. This too reflects the stringent requirements that both ego instincts and sexual instincts place on one another.

The end of Winston's meeting with O'Brien marks the intersection of four important associations in Winston's mind. The first three have to do with Winston's relation to his mother and to Julia, but the latter, curiously, has to do with the image of a church. "Instead of anything directly connected with O'Brien or the Brotherhood, there came into his mind a sort of composite picture of the dark bedroom where his mother had spent her last days, and the little room over Mr. Charrington's shop, and the glass paperweight, and the steel engraving in its rosewood frame" (158). The engraving, depicting St. Clement's Church before it was bombed during the revolution, becomes emblematic of the restoration of Winston's own psyche. For, if Rilke describes the writing of autobiographical prose in terms of the construction of a cathedral, Orwell's vision of the salvation of the self must be seen as a form of postwar reconstruction. The church depicted in the engraving, which Winston recognizes as a ruin next to the Court of Justice, reflects the very state of Winston's own body image; to restore it to its former appearance means re-creating in the language of personal confession the narrative of completeness for which he longs. The image of the church with its "oval building" and "small tower in front" (87) supplies the controlling metaphor for the restored psyche, replicating on the level of architecture the image of a vagina/womb guarded by a phallus. Mr. Charrington's description of St. Martin's Church in Victory Square across from the great victory pillar of Big Brother provides us with an identical impression: "A building with a kind of triangular porch and pillars in front, and a big flight of steps" (88).

If the image of the church depicts the restored psyche on a specular plane, the nursery rhyme enumerating the main churches in London does so at the level of narrative. From the moment that Mr. Charrington furnishes him with the first lines, Winston becomes preoccupied with the rhyme. He derives a curious sense of comfort by attempting to piece the verse together. Even to repeat the nursery rhyme to himself gives him "the illusion of actually hearing bells, the bells of a lost London that still existed somewhere or other, disguised and forgotten. From one ghostly steeple after another he seemed to hear them pealing forth" (89). Through the nursery rhyme Winston is able to re-create the kind of security found in childhood in the lap of a protecting parent, or perhaps the peace found later in adulthood during the repetition of a liturgical prayer in church. Without understanding even the most rudimentary concepts of what these churches once represented, Winston intuitively grasps their psychological function. The very image of the church combines the child's primordial need for a protective womblike space and a guarding authoritative presence; here re-created at the level of architectures is the tropaic/apotropaic structure so necessary to the fulfillment both of the sexual and the self-protective instincts. What we had earlier linked in *Portrait* to Thoth, the Egyptian god of writers, and in the

Notebook to autobiographical writing as the building of a cathedral of self, reappears in Winston's association with image of the church as a herm whose function is to ward off the spirit of Big Brother. It is no accident that St. Clement's stands adjacent to the Court of Law or that St. Martin's stands, disguised as a museum of war relics, directly across from Big Brother's Victory Pillar. Once the original function of these structures is understood, each of these structures becomes a competing herm, intent on creating its own authoritative space. Winston's repetition of the nursery rhyme must therefore be seen as an attempt to invoke the former spirit and psychological function of the church in order to establish the necessary requirements for his own self-sufficiency.

If the image of the church becomes the ideal spatial representation of self-fulfillment and self-protection, the nursery rhyme which Mr. Charrington alludes to and the dance which he describes offer us a narrative key by which we are able to understand Winston's quest to understand and to re-create himself. Winston himself refers to the different stanzas of the rhyme as integral parts of a "countersign." Moreover, the fact that he is able to complete the rhyme only after his encounter with three different characters indicates the importance and interconnection of their roles in the representation of his ego. Charrington not only produces the first lines of the nursery rhyme—"Oranges and lemons, say the bells of St. Clement's"—he also introduces Winston to the material wares by which Winston is able to disobey the party. The "oranges and lemons" sold at his shop include the diary, the glass paperweight, and, finally, a suitably private space, reminiscent of Winston's mother's room, to be used for his liaisons with Julia. In this sense, Charrington is the "prop man" who sets the stage on which the inner drama of Winston's self-actualization is played out to its bitter end. As in the last lines of the rhyme—"Here comes a candle to light you to bed, here comes a chopper to chop off your head"—he knows the beginning and the ending of the drama. For it is Charrington who holds the "candle" that lights Winston to bed, and later, when he turns out to be an agent of the Thought Police, he is also a representative of the "chopper," the harsh, castrating father who comes to chop off Winston's "head."

Julia is next to add a line to the poem: "You owe me three farthings, say the bells of St. Martin's, / When will you pay me? say the bells of Old Bailey" (129). The second line, also remembered by

Mr. Charrington, overlaps with the one Julia recalls, intimating the connection between the bedroom, Winston's mother, and Julia. The subject of payment also calls to mind Winston's rendezvous with the aging prostitute, as it does his necessity of having to pay Mr. Charrington, like a grandfatherly pimp, for the price of the room. Once the "rent" has been paid, Winston is able to find sexual fulfillment through Julia. But Julia is also the one who remembers the refrain about the chopper, intimating that sexual fulfillment stands in a dangerous relation to the harsh, castrating father. Thus, it is only fitting that the remaining undiscovered lines of the poem have to do with authority itself and with its representative, O'Brien. The only question Winston can think of asking O'Brien at the end of their interview, though outwardly trivial, has everything to do with his psychological state. Searching for the final piece in a narrative formula that will aid in the reconstruction of his own psyche, Winston asks O'Brien whether he knows the last line of the nursery rhyme. And O'Brien, as if waiting for the question, is able to comply:

> Oranges and lemons, say the bells of St. Clement's,
> You owe me three farthings, say the bells of St. Martin's,
> When will you pay me? say the bells of Old Bailey,
> When I grow rich, say the bells of Shoreditch. (159)

The culmination of this nursery rhyme reflects Winston's own hopes for the reinstatement of a sense of unity experienced only in childhood. If at the beginning he is offered oranges and lemons, that is, the sweet/sour experience of sexual fulfillment, he discovers that this possibility exacts a price, first for a suitably private space in which it can be fulfilled, but finally at the expense of a part of the self which must be sacrificed for the other. But this price is not paid to Julia, as it was earlier to a prostitute; it must be paid to O'Brien himself. In O'Brien's "countersign" the ego, or "I," is introduced for the first time, suggesting that the offer and payment of the preceding three stanzas and what they are associated with in Winston's relations can be fulfilled only at the expense of the inflation of the "I" represented by O'Brien. The consequences of this choice must therefore be followed by Winston's coming to grips with the meaning and the nature of authority and repression.

The childhood dance attached to the nursery rhyme is also a reflection of the psychic dance going on in Winston's soul. Like the player passing in and out under a circle of linked arms, Winston is attempting to replicate the ring of social relations he experienced in childhood in which he once experienced that "oceanic" feeling of wholeness and security. Charrington, Julia, and O'Brien are external representations of the inner valences which must be approached if he is to reexperience this sense of wholeness. The danger in the game, however, is that by attempting to re-create the internal conditions which he experienced before the "oedipal revolution," he risks an encounter with the "chopper," with its threat of castration by the primal father. To be caught within the linked arms when the nursery rhyme ends is thus both a desired and a dreaded event; it symbolizes both the enclosure within the womb and the symbolic loss of the male organ, both prerequisites so necessary to the reentry into the blissful, preoedipal state. This, then, is the experience which Winston must undergo with O'Brien. As C. M. Kornbluth argues, Winston's entry into the infamous Room 101 is a movement backward through psychic time into the womb, an attempt, in other words, to "burrow into the mother." The numerals "101" in this sense may even, as Kornbluth suggests, "constitute a naive sketch of the female genitalia seen from below" (93). Although Kornbluth may be reading too much into individual symbols, we can speculate that the numerals represent the "rat hole" in Winston's dreams which lead behind that wall of darkness to an event "too dreadful to be faced" (128). In order to achieve the "oceanic" state of being that this "re-entry into the womb" implies, Winston must also make "an intolerably direct confrontation with that prehistoric crime that all of Oceania, of civilization, is organized to suppress and conceal" (Smyer 152).

Apart from their reflection of potential political realities, the ensuing episodes of torture that Winston undergoes with O'Brien in the Ministry of Love must also be viewed as a metaphoric return to and reenactment of the primal scene in which the child first becomes alienated from itself. At this stage the "unified body" which Winston has imagined for himself undergoes the deformation necessary to the establishment of order and authority, not only in the nuclear family, but in what Orwell himself was to call the social family. In order to attempt a return to the childhood state of "oceanic" oneness, Winston must relive the traumatic "dissolution of the Oedipus complex," the process by which desire for the mother becomes linked to the conditional authority of the father. This is not merely the result of a literal process of breaking down the subject's will. It is a process of altering the body image, as we have seen in primitive initiations, so that subjects see themselves as entirely new individuals. In the torture cells of the Ministry of Love, O'Brien slowly destroys Winston's initial body image by beatings, starvation, electrical shocks, and psychological terror. At the end of this ordeal, O'Brien forces Winston to witness his transformation in a triptychlike mirror:

> The creature's face seemed to be protruded, because of its bent carriage. A forlorn, jailbird's face with a nobby forehead running back into a bald scalp, a crooked nose and battered-looking cheekbones above which the eyes were fierce and watchful. The cheeks were seamed, the mouth had a drawn-in look. . . . Except for his hands and a circle of his face, his body was gray all over with ancient, ingrained dirt. Here and there under the dirt there were the red scars of wounds, and near the ankle the varicose ulcer was an inflamed mass with flakes of skin peeling off it. But the truly frightening thing was the emaciation of his body. The barrel of the ribs was as narrow as that of a skeleton; the legs had shrunk so that the knees were thicker than the thighs. . . . The thin shoulders were hunched forward so as to make a cavity of the chest, the scraggy neck seemed to be bending double under the weight of the skull. At a guess he would have said that it was the body of a man of sixty, suffering from some malignant disease. (233–34)

Until O'Brien has forced Winston to look at his body in the mirror, Winston has identified himself with a very different image, one which has remained fixed in his mind, not subject to the decay of disease and age hastened by the techniques of torture. Winston's utter inconsequentiality is suddenly and devastatingly revealed to him; he sees nothing but a dirty, emaciated "bag of filth." In the mechanics of enantiodromia this painful revelation of one's insignificance seems to be a prerequisite to conversion itself and usually corresponds to the image of a tortured or deformed body. St. Augustine, for example, records a similar experience preceding his conversion in his *Confessions:* "But you, Lord, . . . were turning me around so that I could see myself, you took me from behind my own back, which was where I had put myself during the time when I did not want to be observed by myself, and you set me in front of my own face so that I could see how foul a sight I was—crooked, filthy, spotted, and ulcerous" (173). Indeed, when we look at the language of Christian conversion, images of torture abound. We may think of Donne's famous lines, "Batter my heart, three-person'd God." Or we may recall the prayer "Lord grant me a contrite heart"—contrite meaning "crushed" in Latin. But unlike the shocking moment of the recognition of sin in Christianity, Winston's "self-revelation" seems to be occurring both on the outside and on the inside at the same time. What is normally interpreted as an external event—the depiction of human torture in the totalitarian state—becomes a metaphor for an internal process which precedes and in a sense foreshadows the deformation Winston undergoes at the hands of O'Brien.

Winston's ordeal in the Ministry of Love thus spans both past and future. It is a replay of the childhood "initiation" into the "family" hierarchy, but it is also a projection of this particular kind of initiation into the sociopolitical future. At the primal level, this initiation is symbolized by castration, which, according to Freud, is represented in the dreamwork by images such as "baldness, hair-cutting, falling out of teeth, and decapitation" (*Interpretation of Dreams* 385–92). Apparently Orwell did not want the reader to miss the association, for he introduces virtually all the above-mentioned symbols. Not only do we recognize the theme in his allusion to the "chopper" in the nursery rhyme, it becomes more and more apparent in his description of Winston's experience in the Ministry of Love. Directly after the mirror episode, O'Brien plucks a "tuft of hair" out of Winston's balding head. He then commands Winston to open his mouth, pointing out that his "teeth are dropping out of [his] head" (234). In a final gesture, he seizes "one of Winston's remaining front teeth between his powerful thumb and forefinger . . . [wrenches] the loose tooth out by the roots . . . [and tosses] it across the cell" (234).

This symbolic castration might also be linked to the theme of masturbation, which we earlier associated with Julia and with the images of the severed and broken arms. Freud is particularly insistent about relating dreams with a "dental stimulus" to "masturbatory desires of the pubertal period" (385). But he also points out in two dream interpretations that the pulling of teeth in dreams may be indicative of a sublimated homosexuality in which an inhibited desire becomes expressed through a painful activity (386). It may well be the case that Winston's veneration for O'Brien and eventually his love for

Big Brother are a result of a latent homosexuality that links desire with pain. The expression of such compromising sexual imagery accords well with the atmosphere of furtive sexuality and impending punishment in *Nineteen Eighty-Four*, an atmosphere which has reminded more than one critic of Orwell's boarding school days at St. Cyprians. O'Brien often takes on a "school masterish tone" when he is about to administer Winston's punishment, and Julia's appearance—her freckled face, short hair, and "boyish overalls"—suggests a school comrade rather than a female lover. But the images of Julia's masculinity and femininity tend to change frequently, and we are hard put to determine whether she represents any single sexual orientation. She is sex personified, and Winston's attempt to interest her in anything else but her consuming passion is futile. We might even venture to say that she is not so much the object of Winston's desires as the way through which Winston's desires become expressed: desire itself objectivized. Such a sexual relation can only prove dangerous to the social system, regardless of its orientation. "Not merely the love of one person," Winston thinks to himself, "but the animal instinct, the simple undifferentiated desire: that was the force that would tear the Party to pieces" (112). Desire constitutes a threat to the party because it is implicitly onanistic; it wants to project its own objects, and it demands autonomy and wants to remove any obstacle put in its path by authority.

As Foucault argues in his *History of Sexuality*, power and desire are inseparably linked. Only through the specific regulation of desire can the state obtain the energy it needs to function properly. Julia tells Winston: "When you make love you're using up energy; and afterwards you feel happy and don't give a damn for anything. They can't bear you to feel like that. They want you to be bursting with energy all the time. All this marching up and down and cheering and waving flags is simply sex gone sour. If you're happy inside yourself, why should you get excited about Big Brother and the Three-Year Plans and the Two Minutes Hate and all the rest of their bloody rot?" (118). Why indeed? But if the state is attempting to "abolish the orgasm" (230), as O'Brien tells Winston, it is not with the intent to kill desire but to transform it permanently into a new and socially viable form of energy. It is an attempt to turn an originally self-preoccupied and self-inflating instinct into a power which effaces and stands over the self—and this can be achieved only by "reversing the content" of an instinct, a feat which Freud tells us is possible only in the singular instance of "the transformation of love into hate" ("Instincts" 126). O'Brien instructs Winston, "The old civilizations claimed that they were founded on love and justice. Ours is founded upon hatred. In our world there will be no emotions except fear, rage, triumph, and self-abasement" (230). Why should hatred be any more exhausting than love? he asks. The answer may well be that it is not, at least if there is the same possibility of obtaining pleasure from hating as there is from loving. Judging from the "controlled passion" (227), the "lunatic intensity" with which he goes about torturing Winston, O'Brien certainly seems to derive pleasure from his work. "Power is not a means," he tells his victim, "it is an end. . . . The object of persecution is persecution. The object of torture is torture. The object of power is power" (227). As in the conversion of Paul, this "reversal of content," whether from love into hate or vice versa, involves the transference of internal objects—that is to say, the psyche appears to reverse its internal orientation in order to optimize and consolidate its power.

CHAPTER 12

Unified Self / "Docile Body"

If conversion involves a Nietzschean "will to power," this does not answer the question why power may take so many different forms in the mind. According to Foucault, the techniques which Western society uses to link desire with power have grown directly out of the institution of the Christian confession. The way to integrate the sexual instincts into the service of authority, he argues, is to monitor them at every level and to turn them into discourse: "Whether in the form of a subtle confession in confidence, or an authoritarian interrogation, sex—be it refined or rustic—had to be put into words" ("Repressive Hypothesis" 313–14). Ideally, the confession should be desired as much as it is required—that is, it should offer confessants a feeling of release, the deep satisfaction of having unburdened themselves of unwholesome feelings and thoughts. But it must also be a requirement legitimized by a "higher authority" and accepted as a social convention. In *Nineteen Eighty-Four* the institution of the confession is presented from both sides. We recall that it is Winston who voluntarily begins his confession by opening his diary. He feels a compulsion to put into words his innermost thoughts and feelings. He thinks that by confessing himself to an unknown interlocutor, he is freeing himself from the overbearing authority of the state. He wants to project an interlocutor who can combat and neutralize the ominous presence of Big Brother, in spite of the fact that the devices for eliciting and recording confessions—the hidden microphones, the telescreens, the Thought Police, the informants, the instruments of torture—all belong to the state. The likelihood that an alternative authority exists is slim. There are rumors of a competing Brotherhood led by the "primal traitor" Emmanuel Goldstein, but we soon suspect that this "brotherhood" is little more than a popular fantasy, a creation of desire to be used by the state to objectivize and vilify the real primal traitor: desire itself. Nevertheless, the initial autobiographical impulse which comes from Winston is spurred by his belief in the existence of this alternative brotherhood which not only condones prodigality but requires it, not only encourages illicit and promiscuous sexuality but demands it as a "political act." The resulting irony, however, is that this initial autobiographical impulse instigates a process which moves Winston ever nearer to the torture cells of the Ministry of Love.

Strangely enough, the inexorable process that transforms Winston Smith from a novice diarist into a victim of torture does not so much alter the basic need for confession as shift its orientation from that of an autobiographical impulse to that of an authoritarian requirement. For, in the end the impetus for confession comes from O'Brien and not Winston, placing the emphasis on "having to confess" rather than on "wanting to confess." On the surface this appears to be exactly the reverse of what occurs in the conversion of St. Paul. In Paul's case, a sadistic, scopophilic impulse is suddenly turned inward upon itself precisely because the effort to maintain the former orientation was too great. But if we look more closely at the process which leads to Winston's "conversion," we see that there are profound similarities. To understand this relationship more clearly we must return to Freud's discussion of the instincts and their vicissitudes, but we must also consider how the transformations he describes can occur solely as a result of writing about the self. Winston's first entry in his diary consists of the recollection of a scene from a film. We can classify this kind of writing, this reiteration of the observed, as Freud does, as "looking at an extraneous object." But Winston's very choice of scene—the boy's and mother's bodies blown to pieces by an Oceanian bomb—reveals an inner exigency yearning to be called forth. What Winston actually records is his own primal reflection in the observed object, intimating the possibility of a "turning of the scopophilic instinct toward a part of the subject's own body." In this case, as mentioned before, the body part in question is the little boy's detached arm. The recognition of the self in the Other results in a "transformation to passivity and setting up of a new aim—that of being looked at." Only after this transformation has taken place within Winston is he able to introduce a new subject in order to be looked at by him, a reader, identified as O'Brien but in actuality an internal representation of the otherness which Winston must bring to bear on his own confessing self. The sheer need to invent an interlocutor creates the necessity for an internal division and the formulation of a new self as Other.

But this is not all. Once we grasp the internal nature of this transformation to a scopophilia turned inward, we can also trace the relation between writing and sadism. After Winston has recorded his first metaphoric self-revelation, a very different kind of writing emerges. No longer written in a "cramped, childish" style, it issues forth "as though by automatic action," writing "voluptuously" in "large neat capitals." To his astonishment Winston discovers that writing can be a form of violence, a means of retribution—he sees that he has filled nearly half a page with the words "DOWN WITH BIG BROTHER" (20). But since autobiographical writing immediately inverts the self's orientation, it follows that the violence of writing must also be turned inward. Winston as autobiographer becomes his own interlocutor. The more he identifies himself with his role as author/authority of himself, the more he is compelled to question the self, to call it into question, to elicit from it every vestige of truth. The inflation of the authorial "I" is the self's identification with power. It can be achieved only at the expense of the original confessing self, making self-revelation into an increasingly torturous experience. When the writing self takes over, the experiential self becomes its prisoner, a victim of "sadism turned inward upon itself," compelled to confess the crimes attributed to it, whether real or imaginary, and to retreat ever further into the shadow of its interlocutor.

At this point we begin to recognize the parallel between an allegory about the transformation of the confessional self and the conversion of a reserved and diffident Eric Arthur Blair into the intense, visionary writer George Orwell. Peter Stansky and William Abrahams have shown that although the choice of the name George Orwell was arbitrary, the turning of Blair into Orwell involved a "slow, arduous process of transformation" by which "the essential second self, under the name, . . . had been set free" (254). But if the name did not matter, the fact that the "second" writing self had a new name did. Anthony Powell recalls in his memoirs, "I once asked him [Orwell] if he had ever thought of legally adopting his *nom de guerre*. 'Well I have,' he said slowly, 'but then, of course, I'd have to write under another name'" (63). What mattered was that the split between the writing and the experiencing self had been designated. It is the dialectical relation between these two selves which is set forth in *Nineteen Eighty-Four.* More than one critic has remarked upon the curious mixture of biography and fiction in Orwell's work. To be sure, all writers base their fiction on experience to some degree, but Orwell appears to be one of those autobiographical writers who not only borrowed from real life but wrote for the sake of his experience, a fact which his mentor friend Ruth Pitter recognized early in his career (Stansky 187). Moreover, Stansky and Abrahams demonstrate in their literary biography of Eric Blair just how frugal Orwell was with his experiences in using them as materials for his fiction. Orwell clearly had a need to turn experience into fiction and to transform a stock of very personal images into the structural exigencies of a novel. In this sense *Nineteen Eighty-Four* performs the function of the dreamwork by simultaneously revealing and disguising dangerous elements which could otherwise not be brought to light. Like the dreamer, the reader becomes so caught up in the nightmarish plot of the novel that he or she fails to recognize that there are images which by their very persistence or superfluity point to a source outside of the legitimizing framework of the novel—within the mind of the writer surely, but, by extension, within the Western mind as the legacy of the totalizing structure of the Christian confessional tradition.

What makes *Nineteen Eighty-Four* an autobiographical novel, however, is not the fact that it contains autobiographical materials—this condition would implicate all novel writing—but the fact that it traces the fate of the autobiographical impulse with such fidelity. Like a dream which reveals its motives in its very attempt to hide them, it is its author's unflinching portrayal of the inner transformation that takes place when one becomes an author of the self. And finally, it is a projection of the consequences of the need to reveal and justify the self both for individual identity and for social organization. O'Brien and Winston Smith are counterparts of the same person. That is to say, the novel is a confession about a confessing self and a confessor who belong to the same individual. The privileging of O'Brien signals the "successful" initiation of the individual into the social hierarchy, the turning point where the self comes to represent a world of values larger than those initially projected by one's own desire. But we must remember that this process of initiation is inexorably bound up with the projections of desire itself. Winston's quest for salvation is founded on nothing more than a dream; it begins within as a wish. At first O'Brien exists for Winston only as a disembodied voice whispering this promise of salvation to him as he sleeps. But in the end O'Brien has become the dominant image of the self, his justification for authority springing from the depths of the libido, as Freud described in "The Ego and the Id" (39), and transforming itself into the psychic representative of social power, the superego. In the Ministry of Love, Winston acknowledges the superiority of O'Brien's mind, but he also recognizes that he himself belongs to that mind. "O'Brien was a being in all ways larger than himself. There was no idea that he had ever had, or could have, that O'Brien had not long ago known, examined, and rejected. His mind *contained* Winston's mind" (220). O'Brien is taking so much trouble with Winston not only because he is "worth trouble" but because the "Winston Smith" within him must be completely suppressed in order for O'Brien to become the total authority.

Nineteen Eighty-Four is not about the destruction of the self in a totalitarian state; the self cannot be destroyed because it is a fiction. Orwell's novel depicts the reformation this fictional construct "self" must undergo in order to conform to the specific salvational strategy of a confessional tradition as defined by the "imaginary" goals of a specific political vision. It reveals the repressive nature of this tradition both as an internal construct and as a sociopolitical reality. In this sense it is a story about the betrayal of the Christian tradition as it is transmitted by Western culture; the etching of St. Clements Dane screwed to the wall of the upstairs room above Mr. Charrington's "junk shop" only hides the notorious telescreen of the party. Salvation is possible only at the expense of a part of the self which must exist in a suppressed, unconscious state in order to establish and define the ego's sense of authority. The fact that Winston does not receive the "longed-for bullet" at the end of his tortuous interrogation only shows how crucial his continued existence is for a scheme which links desire with power. He must continue to exist in order to fill up the space where the former self had been. He becomes the repressed Other, a burnt-out shell of a man drinking cheap Victory gin and biding his time with chess problems in the Chestnut Cafe in Victory Square. As the repressed Other, he receives a sinecure, that is to say, an ecclesiastical benefice "without cure of souls," a position which requires little or no work and which is "more highly paid than his old job had been" (249). Winston's new job is more highly paid precisely because it is a passive one, the representation of an absence. And as a pure negativity, it performs a key function in the salvational scheme presented in the novel.

Winston's experience in Room 101 can therefore be understood as the final rite de passage in a process of initiation in which one image of the self is replaced by another. At the level of writing, it symbolizes what Paul de Man describes as the "de-facement" which the self must undergo in order to become the subject of autobiography. The cage-mask which O'Brien straps to Winston's face reveals the true underlying function of the "self-life-writing machine"—that of "de-facement," the making over of the subjective face into a face subject to the laws of the signifier. The fact that the threat of defacement is carried out by rats indicates just how this process is connected to the primal scene. The rat symbolizes the violence of the phallus/signifier itself which O'Brien, who represents the harsh castrating father, now has in his possession. For Winston, the problem of salvation is that he must become incorporated by this signifier/phallus in order to achieve the longed-for state of Oceanic oneness. To paraphrase Lacan, the desire of the mother is translated into the desire to become the phallus for the mother. However, Winston cannot achieve this state simply by ceasing to exist. As previously mentioned, his existence as suppressed Other is an essential part of the salvational scheme. He can be saved only by giving up his most precious possession, the very symbol of his desire, Julia, that particularly "boyish" girl who has already had her "arm" broken by the "novel-writing machine." Once the masklike apparatus has been installed and didactically explained by O'Brien, Winston can never be the same. He has internalized that image of the future which O'Brien has depicted as "a boot stamping on a human face—forever" (230). But we must also remember that when Winston is released from the Ministry of Love, he has a new face: "his features had thickened, the skin on nose and cheekbones was coarsely red, even the bald scalp was too deep a pink" (249). And more telling, "they had pulled out the remnants of his teeth and given him a new set of dentures" (237). Even his teeth now belong to the state. One might almost imagine this new face to have grown closer in resemblance to the coarse, fleshy face of his tormentor, protector, inquisitor, and friend, O'Brien.

The Christian symbolism in *Nineteen Eighty-Four* has been noted by several critics, usually with the contention that elements like the worship of Big Brother and O'Brien's catechismal initiation are ironic elements intended to satirize modern religion. Certainly this is true. But such claims are not incompatible with the notion that the novel also depicts a serious quest for identity whose images conform to an "age-old symbolic structure, and even phraseology, of resistant man's breakdown and conversion to God" (Gerber 41). Moreover, while disputing that this pattern also reflects an unconscious attitude, William Empson argues that the motif of religious conversion in the novel should be taken literally—as a warning: "Surely Orwell made very clear that he considered it the ultimate shame for a man to hand over his conscience either to Stalin the Big Brother or to . . . God the Father. . . . Surely the conception of a Ministry of Love, whose towering office hagrides the city because each citizen believes it has calculated for him the torture he would find most unbearable, corresponds to nothing in Communism and a great deal in the history of Christianity" (41). But what Empson does not consider is that Orwell may not so much have been criticizing the Christian tradition as bemoaning the fact that it had lost its former power to save the soul of the individual from the crushing power of the state. As George Woodcock observes, "Orwell regretted that the young people in the generation growing up around him had lost that knowledge of the Bible which at one time was one of the most precious possessions of Englishmen." Furthermore, "Orwell realized that there was a natural cohesion and common sense of purpose in every religious age which secular societies would be able to reproduce only with difficulty, and then probably in the wrong ways—'the glittering Utopias and ant heaps of steel and concrete' to which he looked forward with nausea" (139).

Nineteen Eighty-Four can be understood as a parable of salvation performed in a demotic world. Winston is the quintessentially modern prodigal seeking freedom in a world in which language no longer fulfills its former unifying, transcendental function. Winston's quest therefore can result only in a metaphor of a literal action. As Orwell accurately observed in his epilogue "The Principles of Newspeak," the central problem of finding individual salvation in the world of *Nineteen Eighty-Four* was that language was somehow being tampered with and that people had no alternative but to conform to the language world into which they were born. But it was not merely the fact that the modern world had consciously reduced the possibility for creating unauthorized meanings at the political level; it was the fact that a long-standing rational struggle against religious authority had robbed language of its traditionally unifying structures, making it predominantly a descriptive tool. Thereafter, if a unity did indeed exist, it had to exist as an objective reality before it could be translated into language. In such a world Winston is unable to create a saving metaphysical construct. He cannot believe in God, but neither can he define the inner spirit that will rebel against the political authority of Ingsoc. Paradoxically, he attempts to solve his dilemma by invoking the traditional Christian program for salvation—taking on the role of the prodigal son who rejects the "father" and seeks his own form of authority on the road of his desires. Like the prodigal, Winston must inevitably return "home," but this time not merely because he cannot continue on his path alone but because he cannot escape his language world. It belongs to him; indeed, it is in him. The difficulty remains that in this demotic world there is no benevolent father to greet and forgive him, no celebration and no slaughtered lamb. Too much time has passed. The father/God is dead. The older brother has inherited the "farm." And Big Brother remembers a previous occasion when he was cheated out of his inheritance, when the Father disparaged his obedience and toil by accepting the prodigal back as a Son. This time, however, he knows it will be different because *he* is the representative of the absent father, the father who was murdered so long ago and whose murder could find no atonement but the raising up of a benevolent, forgiving father in language. This time, however, there will be no forgiveness.

IV

Conclusions

CHAPTER 13

Epitome: The Dream of Salvation

In the beginning men and women lived in a dreamlike world. The objects around them, their sensations, and even the words they spoke were like the images of a dream. They lived in their language like sleepers live in dreams, encountering every hieroglyphic image as a literal and magical reality. What came from within was identical to that which came from without. Whether they merely heard the word or whether it was inscribed on their bodies made no difference. Their response to this word was literal and unequivocal. Initiation into the group was therefore an initiation into a communal dream in which all inscriptions held the same meanings for everyone. Initiation was the standardization of the dream.

Eventually the sleepers awoke from their dream. As their eyes began to focus on the world around them, they realized that they had been sleeping and that the sense of unity which they had previously experienced had been only an illusion. Awake, they were no longer actors within their own dream. They could not re-create the sense of total belonging they had felt at the level of the dream language. They felt a deep nostalgia for this previous existence and wanted to return to the world of sleep. They realized, moreover, that in the dream unity they had known, they and those around them were given together. They were part of the same dream. Now they saw that they did not belong together and that each of them was alone. Even their bodies no longer belonged to them as they had before. All this because the image had become separated from the "text" of the dream. Initiation lost its absolute inevitability and became a rhetorical act.

Gradually the awakened sleepers discovered that language itself offered the possibility of a unity of thought and that by putting together words in a particular way, they were able to persuade others of this unity. Thus, although a literal return to the "unconscious" state of the dream was out of the question, it became possible for each individual to re-create an ideal unity consciously by putting together words in the appropriate manner. Initiation became a matter of "conversion," of accepting and identifying with a verbal unity which came from outside the self. Language acquired both a religious and a political dimension in that it became the very means by which individuals were unified, by which their disparities were gathered up into hierarchized units of ideality. At the same time, this ideational language was a personal possession people could carry with them regardless of the situation in which they found themselves. Inscription itself became mobilized, less permanent, more flexible, demanding a more internalized approach to the conception of identity.

But there were difficulties. The awakened dreamers faced the problem of reconciling the personal language of their dream with the hieratic form of language that they were now forced to accept as their possession. Some kind of mechanism of mediation had to be established, and in the Christian world that mechanism was the confession. By creating two subjects in a discourse of denial and affirmation—the confessing self representing the old dreaming self and the interlocuting self representing the new authorizing, verbal self—the awakened dreamers were able to set into motion a process by which they could both pacify their longing for their dream world and, at the same time, identify with the authorizing unity presented to them by language. The longed-for dream world became preserved (*aufgehoben*) in the form of a negation in a social discourse of self-justification. Conversion therefore necessarily involved images of torture and deformation; in order that the "body" of the dreamer be preserved, its presence had to be justified by pain. Thus, the metaphor of the mutilation of the human body became a reenactment of the primitive ritual inscription at the level of language in which a primary hieroglyphic writing was subsumed by a logos-centered rhetorical script. But the awakened dreamers gradually realized that they were paying a high price for their sense of unity by trying to recreate it at the level of language. They saw how groups were using verbal constructions to their advantage and how a gap was opening up between the dream world and the waking social world. In their daily activities they recognized how the logocentric language they had accepted did not necessarily correspond to their experience. It did not, for example, explain external phenomena (which they were already interpreting by other means), nor did it mollify their inner discontentment. Gradually, they recognized the possibility of using a new, descriptive form of language, the language of science and commerce, to combat the false and compromising rhetoric of tradition. The breakdown of one authorizing tradition meant the establishment of a new authorizing language, one which did not depend on a hierarchical system of valuation and could be more easily defended and employed by the individual.

What followed was unforeseeable. This new descriptive language, once successful in its bid for authority, was unable to re-create the unity once experienced by the dreamer. It could only analyze and describe events, could only reflect logical unities occurring outside of itself. To reproduce the more totalizing state of unity and self-justification, the individual had to fall back on the old techniques of the confession and conversion, only this time the space allotted for the interlocuting, authorizing self was empty and had to be filled by the individual discourse. Invariably, the image projected into this space took the form of a reader—urbane, rational, intelligent, and empathetic. Above all empathetic. For the salvation of the secular confessional self depended solely on the correspondences set up between one subject and another, on the mutual interchangeability of these subjects. The secular confessing self may have delivered itself up to this reader, to whom it exposed its most hidden secrets and for whose pleasure it tortured itself in order to obtain the grace that comes from unburdening oneself to another. But the sought-for absolution did not come from the reader. It resulted from a refined process of inversion or substitution by which the identifying reader was lured into the place of the confessing self and thus mastered by the author. By establishing this intimate form of correspondence, autobiographical authors were able to put themselves in a position of authority, not only over themselves but over others. Pushing self-revelation to its limits, the writers of the self created a mutilating rite by which they could initiate those outside of themselves into their own totalizing world. In its very audacity their confession challenged the prevailing social norms which forbade it, projecting a more powerful *imaginary* authority-figure beyond the established limits of the world around them. Inevitably, even this "metafather figure" had to be seen for what it really was—the projection of the totalizing desire of the dream, the unconscious wish for mastery.

CHAPTER 14

Epilogue: Kafka's "Nightmare"

> "Our sentence does not sound severe. Whatever commandment the prisoner has disobeyed is written upon his body by the Harrow. This prisoner, for instance" — the officer indicated the man — "will have written on his body: HONOR THY SUPERIORS!" — (Kafka, "In the Penal Colony")

IN KAFKA'S "In the Penal Colony" the theme of human mutilation as a ritual writing on the body finds its most graphic image: a writing machine so refined that the effect of its exquisitely prolonged torture is a form of recognition and salvation, a self-reading of the inscriptions on the body of the condemned through the pain it produces on his body. It is a situation so bizarre that we immediately relegate it to a special category of nightmare — the Kafkaesque. But the prototypes of Kafka's writing machine are not merely to be sought in some ancestral "dream time," or in the hieroglyphic world of the Old Testament, or in the tortuous dualism of a St. Augustine. This is *our* nightmare (to paraphrase Joyce's Stephen Dedalus), one from which we are still trying to wake up.

Learning language is the universalizing act of inscription. To speak means to submit to the laws of the signifier. Whether hieroglyphic, hieratic, or demotic, language centers us in the interactive structure of the community. The difference between one mode and the next lies in the way this centeredness is achieved and experienced. To have an identity within language means to be marked by the limitations of an authorizing inscription; one submits the "imaginary" body to a systematic dismemberment and reconstitution into the body of the "socialized" self. Some of these marks are so deeply inscribed in the discourse of our culture as to appear natural and not part of the visible cultural order. Such socializing marks lie at the very heart of the structure of possible social relations, prescribing not only the limits but the very conditions of our behavior and thought. We can experience the limiting power of these "ur" inscriptions only at moments of transgression or wishfulness and thus usually at the level of suffering; we "read" the negative imprint of what language imposes on our bodies.

These "ur" inscriptions are constantly being redeployed to lend authority at the most irrational level to newer authorizing discourses. Old and new socializing inscriptions are aligned through the temporal organizations that link them together. The master narrative of conversion must be understood as one of several unifying devices which align the person with the community and with the authorizing inscriptions within that community. It has an *operational function* through which we articulate the magical transition from the imaginary body to the socialized body. In this sense it not only reestablishes the unity of identity experienced in the imaginary body; it links this identity to the specific figural strategies in language which mark the individual's place within the dominant social discourse. The story of Kafka's "writing apparatus" illustrates the inevitable position of consciousness caught within this dialectical operation between the imaginary body and the law of the signifier.

Gilles Deleuze and Felix Guattari observe that "In the Penal Colony" "presents the law as a pure and empty form without content, the object of which remains unknowable: thus the law can be expressed through a sentence and the sentence can be learned only through a punishment" (43). The conversion narrative *is* an empty form made up of inscriptions imported from the most primitive socialization practices. This form, so emptied of its originary content, can be filled by any number of new values. It may be employed equally by those identifying with the dominant social order or by those marginalized by it who identify with groups asserting their own autonomy and self-legitimacy.

Indeed, the poststructuralist move beyond the relation which centers the subject in social language toward an affirmation of fragmentation and the relativity of discursive "play" is viewed with some suspicion by some feminist and cultural critics. Rather than offering a means of critiquing the dominant cultural order, it is seen as an attempt by its defenders to withhold the very unifying strategy that would empower the marginalized person. Thus, at every level, the individual accepts the totalizing operation for the sake of the legitimizing communality it produces. But the limitations the communal discourse ultimately imposes do not, in themselves, legitimize the authority of the community. For this we must receive something more in return. We must be made to feel at home in the socialized order, protected from both within and without. We must be promised an identity which gives us full membership status within the collective and thus avoid the social death of silence or exclusion.

The question remains, What happens to the promise of the totalizing narrative, what vicissitudes must it undergo, when the belief in a logocentric, metaphysical authority disappears? As I have tried to show, the idea of conversion becomes problematized because of the shift in the way language is used. For the modern autobiographer who understands language primarily on a demotic level, the ground for a belief in a metaphysical, logos-centered authority has fallen away. This implies the loss of a significant unifying dimension and calls the entire mechanism of self-scrutiny and confession into question. Foucault, for example, argues that the entire Christian tradition of the confession has fallen prey to an ever-centralizing and constricting network of political power relationships. A mechanism once connected to metaphysical verities has become enmeshed in the totalizing web of state or corporate power. Paradoxically, individuals who believe they are liberating themselves from external authority by confessing their individuality are only making themselves subject to the kind of authority they are trying to overcome.

But the danger may be even more insidious. The narrative of conversion, like other totalizing strategies, also may be implicated in a process of isolating specific cultural forms of authority from the centralizing political and economic power relationships. Although society may be in the process of becoming more unified at the geopolitical level, it is also becoming more culturally and politically fragmented as various interpretive communities seek to attain their autonomy through the very totalizing strategies they repudiate at the more encompassing level. Confessional writers more consciously aim their work at specific publics in a process of reciprocal legitimization. Thus, in the name of cultural, sexual, or racial empowerment, the conversion narrative becomes the very means by which more complex, superior cultural unities become forestalled. What remains is a loose, mutually exclusive federation of cultural or ideological units linked only by a common economic destiny not unlike the segregated distribution of species in the exhibitionistic economy of a state zoo. It is difficult to predict the durability of such an economic and voyeuristic totality. Certainly it cannot be maintained without invoking deep social divisions, even perpetuating various forms of identity on the basis of these divisions. This is not to say that such totalizing narratives are not effective or necessary political tools, but they do have inherent limitations in defining subsequent stages of identity formation in which the subject produces itself vis-à-vis a more encompassing, superior social vision.

In Kafka's story, however, the writing machine falls apart completely because the authority on which it was based has eroded away: "The machine was apparently falling to pieces; its smooth operation was an illusion" (165). As the lid of the Designer apparatus "click[s] wide open" and one cogwheel after another is forced out, "as if some enormous force were squeezing the Designer" (164), even the condemned man forgets his plight and tries to catch the pieces as they fall out of the machine. In a desperate move, the officer then *takes the place of the victim*, eager to demonstrate the "salvational" effect of this age-old sacrificial operation. Nevertheless, the longed-for redemption does not occur: "this was no exquisite torture such as the officer desired, this was plain murder" (165). In the end, salvation becomes impossible because the power to be saved no longer exists: "It was as it had been in life; no sign was visible of the promised redemption" (166). As Foucault points out, the confession's "veracity is not guaranteed by the lofty authority of the magistery, nor by the tradition it transmits, but by the bond, the basic intimacy in discourse between the one who speaks and what he is speaking about" (*History of Sexuality* 62). If the intimate bond between the speaker and the spoken is severed, then any form of salvation becomes impossible. The machine and the social order on which it was based break down.

In Deleuze and Guattari's assessment Kafka's machine "is still too connected to overly Oedipal coordinates (the commandant—officer = father—son)" and therefore is unable to develop; that is, it cannot turn into a novel but must fall "back into the level of a story" (39). But this would appear to be precisely its function, to set limits and to regulate the production of desire within the oedipal boundaries, inhibiting an internal renovation of social interaction by positing an endless repetition of "stories," the only alternative to which is exclusion or escape from the island colony. Joyce's *Portrait*, for example, presents just this failed attempt to flee the hieratic island of Irish Catholicism by reestablishing in *symbolic terms* an imaginary unity based on a historically archaic metafather image. Rilke's *Notebook*, by contrast, might be understood as a renovation of the island identity (as seen in Malte's tapestry interpretations) by forestalling the totalizing law of the symbolic father. Through this process of deferral a projected imaginary other is allowed to gather itself so that, through its corroborative power in the reading consciousness, it may at least temporarily stand in the place of the symbolic father, offering the possibility of a more spacious mode of being. Both Rilke's novel and Orwell's *Nineteen Eighty-Four* in effect argue that, in the modern, demotic world, the function of autobiographical writing is to help the writing self *abstain* from conversions, since these are apt to involve transitions not from an imaginary world to a symbolic one but to symbolic displacements of the imaginary order (as with the promise of totalitarian states). In Orwell's novel, the promise of an escape from or alteration of the totalizing salvational model through self-writing ultimately is not fulfilled. What began as a liberating strategy ends up, in Foucaultian terms, and as Winston Smith represents at the end of his ordeal, a "docile body."

According to Kafka's illustration, alteration of the communal/individual model of identity is a tenuous proposition at best. Although the "new commandant" of the penal colony is no longer in sympathy with the system, he seems powerless to be able to change it from the inside; it remains for the system to fall apart of its own accord as it reaches the final stages of an intolerable paranoia. It seems questionable, therefore, whether the reader of culture can ever truly escape the inherent violence of the signifier into the kind of "lethetic reading" or Derridean play that Clayton Koelb argues for in his discussion of Kafka's work. More likely, this playful form of interpretation suggests that readers are already inscribed in a superior discourse, one which exempts them from the fundamental law of the discourse in which they immerse themselves.

The intransigence of the oedipal construct within this scenario might therefore be indicative of a persistent attitude toward language, one that has not fundamentally changed even at the most descriptive/demotic level. Freud's mythical scenario, outlined in *Totem and Taboo,* briefly recapitulated, reads thus: the sons who desire the mother discover that the father stands between them and their love-object. As a result, they band together and do away with the father, thus achieving their original aim. This "primal" murder, however, inaugurates an overwhelming guilt, which can be appeased only by setting up an image of father-authority in language to which they pay homage. The system of prohibitions and regulations which grows out of this pact, with its rules of property and exchange, is the beginning of human culture in the sense that we know it.

But Freud's myth of the primal father need not be understood only as a literal myth of origin. It is a retrospective projection of our relation to language. What Freud described as a relation to the mother might thus be considered our imaginary attachment to our own bodies; the conflict between the son and the father, only a reification of the effects of our "alienation into the signifying chain." If the authority which inserts itself between the individual and his or her desires is always an encoded one, the law, the logos, then the individual's identity becomes subject to the repressive, hierarchizing forces that language exerts. In this sense we must dispense with the idea that language is available to everyone in the same way. Human identity is figural, and figuration is rhetorical in character. Language, moreover, as Bakhtin has shown us, is in conflict with itself, and identity is obtained by allying oneself with specific figural strategies on this linguistic battlefield. What needs to be written is a rhetoric of the metaphor in this constitution of human identity. In one way or another, we are always subjected to the inherent violence of the signifying system. To repudiate our own identity involves a rejection of the signifying order into which we are inscribed. At this level the primal murder that Freud spoke of becomes nothing less than the desecration of the symbolic chain, the destruction of the bond between speaker and the spoken. If the overcoming of fatherly authority involves guilt, then it is guilt against language, sin against the signifier itself. A loving relationship to the "signifying father" can therefore be preserved only by the redesignation of authority in the symbols themselves. This redesignation of authority is never merely the replacing of one object with another; it entails the redefinition of the ground of authority, a reformulation from the possibilities offered by language in order to escape the figural net that confines us. Nevertheless, our bond with language, once broken, must always be reestablished. It is in this sense that human salvation always implies a return and that Jesus' parable of the prodigal son is paradigmatic. We are all children of the signifier. To be forgiven our transgression against language, we must either resubmit ourselves to its laws or be able to conceive a language by which we authorize our own forgiveness.

Works Consulted

Altieri, Charles. "Wordsworth's 'Preface' as Literary Theory." *Criticism* 18.2 (Spring 1976): 122–46.

Augustine of Hippo. *The Confessions of St. Augustine.* Trans. Rex Warner. New York: New American Library, 1963.

Baillie, John. *Baptism and Conversion.* New York: Charles Scribner's Sons, 1963.

Baron, Frank, Ernst Dick, and Warren R. Maurer. *Rainer Maria Rilke: The Alchemy of Alienation.* Lawrence: Regents Press of Kansas, 1980.

Beauvoir, Simon de. "Must We Burn Sade?" Trans. Annette Michelson. In *The Marquis de Sade.* Ed. and trans. Austryn Wainhouse and Richard Seaver. New York: Grove Press, 1966. 3–64.

Berger, Peter L., ed. *The Other Side of God: A Polarity in World Religions.* Garden City: Anchor Press/Doubleday, 1981.

Berggren, Erik. *The Psychology of Confession.* Leiden: E. J. Brill, 1975.

Bettelheim, Bruno. *Freud and Man's Soul.* New York: Alfred A. Knopf, 1983.

Betz, Maurice. *Rilke in Frankreich: Erinnerungen, Briefe, Dokumente.* Vienna: Herbert Reichner Verlag, 1938.

Borchardt, Hans Heinrich. "Das Problem des 'Verlorenen Sohnes' bei Rilke." In *Worte und Werte. Bruno Markwardt zum 60. Geburtstag.* Berlin: n.p., 1961. 24–33.

Brereton, Virginia Lieson. *From Sin to Salvation: Stories of Women's Conversions, 1800 to the Present.* Bloomington: Indiana Univ. Press, 1991.

Brown, Russel E. *Index zu Rainer Maria Rilkes "Die Aufzeichnungen des Malte Laurids Brigge."* Indices zur deutschen Literatur 6. Frankfurt am Main: Athenäum Verlag, 1971.

Bruss, Elizabeth. *Autobiographical Acts: The Changing Situation of a Literary Genre.* Baltimore: Johns Hopkins Univ. Press, 1976.

Buckley, Jerome Hamilton. "The Pattern of Conversion." In *The Victorian Temper: A Study in Literary Culture.* Cambridge: Harvard Univ. Press, 1951.

———. *The Turning Key: Autobiography and the Subjective Impulse since 1800.* Cambridge: Harvard Univ. Press, 1984.

Buddeberg, Else. *Rainer Maria Rilke: Eine innere Biographie.* Stuttgart: J. B. Metzlersche Verlagsbuchhandlung, 1954.

Budge, A. Wallis. *The Gods of the Egyptians.* Vol. 1. New York: Dover Publications, 1969.

Burckhardt, Jacob. *The Civilization of the Renaissance in Italy.* Trans. S. G. C. Middlemore. N.p.: Albert and Charles Boni, 1935.

Burkert, Walter. *Structure and History in Greek Mythology and Ritual.* Berkeley: Univ. of California Press, 1979.

Cardan, Jerome. *The Book of My Life (De Vita Propria Liber).* Trans. Jean Stoner. New York: Dover Publications, 1962.

Carlyle, Thomas. *Sartor Resartus and Selected Prose.* New York: Holt, Rinehart and Winston, 1970.

Coe, Richard N. *When the Grass Was Taller: Autobiography and the Experience of Childhood.* New Haven: Yale Univ. Press, 1984.

Daim, Wilfried, M.D. *Depth Psychology and Salvation.* Trans. and ed. Kurt F. Reinhardt. New York: Frederick Ungar Publishing, 1963.

Davidson, William L. *The Stoic Creed.* New York: Arno Press, 1979.

Deleuze, Gilles, and Felix Guattari. *Kafka: Toward a Minor Literature.* Minneapolis: Univ. of Minnesota Press, 1986.

De Luca, V. A. *Thomas DeQuincey: The Prose of Vision.* Toronto: Univ. of Toronto Press, 1980.

De Man, Paul. "Autobiography as De-Facement." In *The Rhetoric of Romanticism.* New York: Columbia Univ. Press, 1984.

De Quincey, Thomas. *The Collected Writings of Thomas De Quincey.* Ed. David Masson, 14 vols. Edinburgh: A. and C. Black, 1889–90.

De Quincey, Thomas. *Confessions of an Opium Eater and Other Writings.* Ed. Aileen Ward. New York: n.p., 1966.

Derrida, Jacques. "Freud and the Scene of Writing." *Yale French Studies* 48 (1972): 73–117.

——. *Of Grammatology.* Baltimore: Johns Hopkins Univ. Press, 1976.

——. "Plato's Pharmacy." In *Dissemination.* Chicago: Univ. of Chicago Press, 1981.

——. "Structure, Sign, and Play in the Discourse of the Human Sciences." In *Writing and Difference.* Chicago: Univ. of Chicago Press, 1978.

——. White Mythology: Metaphor in the Text of Philosophy." In *Margins of Philosophy.* Trans. Alan Bass. Chicago: Univ. of Chicago Press, 1982.

De Singuença, Fray Joseph. *Tercera parte de la Historia de la Orden de S. Gerónimo.* Madrid, 1605.

Dettmering, Peter. *Dichtung und Psychoanalyse: Thomas Mann, Rainer Maria Rilke, Richard Wagner.* Munich: Nymphenburger Verlagshandlung, 1969.

Doubrovsky, Serge. "Autobiographie/Verité/Psychanalyse." *L'Esprit Créateur.* Fall 1980: 87–97.

Durkheim, Emile. *The Elementary Forms of Religious Life.* Trans. Joseph Ward Swain. London: George Allen and Unwin, 1964.

Eakin, Paul John. *Fictions in Autobiography: Studies in the Art of Self Invention.* Princeton: Princeton Univ. Press, 1985.

Earl, William. *The Autobiographical Consciousness: A Philosophical Inquiry into Existence.* Chicago: Quadrangle Books, 1972.

Egan, Susan. *Patterns of Experience in Autobiography.* Chapel Hill: Univ. of North Carolina Press, 1984.

Eliade, Mircea. *The Myth of the Eternal Return.* Bollingen Series 46. New York: Pantheon, 1954.

——. *Rites and Symbols of Initiation: The Mysteries of Birth and Rebirth.* New York: Harper and Row, 1965.

Ellmann, Richard. *The Consciousness of Joyce.* London: Faber and Faber, 1977.

——. *James Joyce.* London: Oxford Univ. Press, 1982.

Empson, William. "Correspondence." *Critical Quarterly* 1 (1959): 41.

Felman, Shoshana. "To Open the Question." In *Literature and Psychoanalysis: The Question of Reading: Otherwise.* Ed. Felman. Baltimore: Johns Hopkins Univ. Press, 1982. 5–10.

Fisch, Max Harold. Introduction. "Portia's Proposal." In *The Autobiography of Giambattista Vico.* Trans. M. H. Fisch and T. G. Bergin. Ithaca: Cornell Univ. Press, 1944.

Foucault, Michel. *The History of Sexuality. Vol. 1: An Introduction.* New York: Vintage Books, 1980.

——. *Nietzsche, Genealogy, History, Language, Counter Memory, Practice: Selected Essays and Interviews.* Ithaca: Cornell Univ. Press, 1977.

——. "On the Genealogy of Ethics: An Overview of Work in Progress." In *The Foucault Reader.* Ed. Paul Rabinow. New York: Pantheon Books, 1984.

——. "The Repressive Hypothesis." In *The Foucault Reader.* Ed. Paul Rabinow. New York: Pantheon Books, 1984.

——. *Le souci de soi. Histoire de la sexualité.* Paris: Gallimard, 1984.

——. "The Subject and Power." In *Michel Foucault: Beyond Structuralism and Hermeneutics.* By Hubert Dreyfus and Paul Rabinow. Chicago: Univ. of Chicago Press, 1977.

Fraenger, Wilhelm. "The Millennium: Outlines of an Interpretation." In *Hieronymus Bosch.* New York: Dorset Press, 1983.

Frazer, Sir James. *Totem and Exogamy: A Treatise on Certain Early Forms of Superstition and Society.* London: Macmillan, 1910.

Freud, Sigmund. "The Antithetical Meaning of Primal Words." *SE* 11:153–61. (See *SE* below.)

——. *Beyond the Pleasure Principle. SE* 18:7–64.

——. "The Claims of Psychoanalysis to the Interest of Non-Psychological Sciences." *SE* 13:165–90.

——. "The Dissection of the Psychical Personality (Lecture 31)." In *New Introductory Lectures on Psychoanalysis. SE* 22:57–80.

——. "Dostoevsky and Parricide." *SE* 21:173–94.

——. "Dream Interpretation as an Illustration." In *An Outline of Psychoanalysis. SE* 23:165–71.

——. "The Ego and the Id and Other Works." *SE* 19:12–66.

——. "Freud to Fliess (Letter 69)." *SE* 1:259–60.

——. "Instincts and Their Vicissitudes." *SE* 14:117–40.

——. *The Interpretation of Dreams. SE* 4–5.

——. *Leonardo da Vinci and a Memory of His Childhood. SE* 11:63–137.

——. *Moses and Monotheism: An Outline of Psychoanalysis and Other Works. SE* 23:3–137.

——. "A Note upon the Mystic Writing Pad." *SE* 19:227–32.

——. "Project for a Scientific Psychology." *SE* 1:295–397.

——. "Symbolism in Dreams." In *Introductory Lectures on Psychoanalysis. SE* 15:149–69.

——. *Three Essays on the Theory of Sexuality. SE* 7:125.

——. *Totem and Taboo. SE* 13:1–161.

Frye, Northrop. *Anatomy of Criticism.* Princeton: Princeton Univ. Press, 1973.

——. *The Great Code: The Bible and Literature.* New York: Harcourt, Brace, Jovanovich, 1982.

Fülleborn, Ulrich. "Form und Sinn der *Aufzeichnungen des Malte Laurids Brigge.*" In *Untersuchungen zu Aufbau und Aussagegehalt der "Aufzeichnungen des Malte Laurids Brigge" von Rainer Maria Rilke.* Rheinfelden: Schäuble, 1983.

Gerber, Richard. "The English Island Myth: Remarks Upon the Englishness of Utopian Fiction." *Critical Quarterly* 1 (1959).

Goethe, Johann Wolfgang von. *Wilhelm Meister's Apprenticeship.* Trans. Thomas Carlyle. New York: Collier Books, 1962.

Graff, W. L. *Rainer Maria Rilke: Creative Anguish of a Modern Poet.* Princeton: Princeton Univ. Press, 1956.

Gunn, Janet Varner. *Autobiography: Towards a Poetics of Experience.* Philadelphia: Univ. of Pennsylvania Press, 1982.

Gusdorf, Georges. "Conditions and Limits of Autobiography." In *Autobiography: Essays Theoretical and Critical.* Ed. James Olney. Princeton: Princeton Univ. Press, 1980. 28–48.

Hamburger, Käte. "Die Geschichte des Verlorenen Sohnes bei Rilke." In *Studies in German in Memory of Robert L. Kahn.* Ed. Hans Eichner and Lisa Kahn. *Rice Univ. Studies* 57. 4 (Fall 1971): 55–71.

——. *Rilke, eine Einführung.* Stuttgart: Ernst Klett Verlag, 1976.

Hart, Francis R. "Notes for an Anatomy of Modern Autobiography." *New Literary History* 1 (Spring 1970).

Hegel, G. W. F. *The Phenomenology of Mind.* New York: Harper and Row, 1967.

Heidegger, Martin. *On the Way to Language.* New York: Harper and Row, 1982.

——. *Unterwegs zur Sprache.* Pfüllingen: Verlag Günter Neske, 1959.

Hicks, R. D. *Stoic and Epicurean.* New York: Charles Scribner's Sons, 1910.

Horace. *The Complete Works of Horace.* Ed. Casper J. Kraemer, Jr. New York: Modern Library, 1936.

Horowitz, Irving. "Autobiography as the Presentation of Self for Social Immortality." *New Literary History* 9.1 (Autumn 1977): 173–77.

Howarth, William L. "Some Principles of Autobiography." In *Autobiography: Essays Theoretical and Critical.* Ed. James Olney. Princeton: Princeton Univ. Press, 1980. 84–114.

Imhof, Heinrich. *Rilke's "Gott": Rainer Maria Rilke's Gottesbild als Spiegelung des Unbewussten.* Poesie und Wissenschaft 22. Heidelberg: Lothar Stiehm Verlag, 1983.

James, William. *The Varieties of Religious Experience.* New York: Penguin Books, 1982.

Jameson, Fredric. *The Political Unconscious.* Ithaca: Cornell Univ. Press, 1981.

Jay, Paul. *Being in the Text: Self-Representation from Wordsworth to Roland Barthes.* Ithaca: Cornell Univ. Press, 1984.

Jaynes, Julian. *The Origin of Consciousness in the Breakdown of the Bicameral Mind.* Boston: Houghton Mifflin, 1976.

Jensen, Ejner J., ed. *The Future of Nineteen Eighty-Four.* Ann Arbor: Univ. of Michigan Press, 1984.

Joyce, James. *The Critical Writings of James Joyce*. Ed. Elsworth Mason and Richard Ellmann. London: Faber and Faber, 1959.

——. *A Portrait of the Artist as a Young Man*. New York: Viking Press, 1965.

——. *Stephen Hero*. Ed. Theodore Spenser. New York: New Directions, 1963.

——. *Ulysses*. New York: Vintage Books, 1961.

Jung, C. G. *Archetypes and the Collective Unconscious*. Trans. R. F. C. Hull. Bollingen Series 20. Princeton: Princeton Univ. Press, 1980.

Kafka, Franz. *The Complete Stories*. New York: Schocken Books, 1971.

——. "In der Strafkolonie." In *Erzählungen*. Frankfurt: Fischer Verlag, 1983.

Kant, Immanuel. *Critique of Judgement*. Trans. J. H. Bernard. New York: Hafner Library of Classics, 1951.

Kee, Howard Clark. "The Conversion of Paul: Confrontation or Interiority." In *The Other Side of God: A Polarity in World Religions*. Ed. Peter L. Berger. Garden City: Anchor Press/Doubleday, 1981.

Koelb, Clayton. "The Margin in the Middle: Kafka's Other Reading of Reading." In *Kafka and the Contemporary Critical Performance*. Bloomington: Indiana Univ. Press, 1987.

Kornbluth, C. M. "The Failure of the Science Fiction Novel as Social Criticism." In *The Science Fiction Novel, Imagination, and Social Criticism*. Ed. Basil Davenport. Chicago: Advent Publishers, 1959.

Kristeva, Julia. "Women's Time." In *Critical Theory since 1965*. Ed. Hazard Adams. Tallahassee: Florida State Univ. Press, 1986. 469–84.

Lacan, Jacques. *Écrits: A Selection*. Trans. Alan Sheridan. New York: W. W. Norton, 1977.

——. *Speech and Language in Psychoanalysis*. Ed. and trans. Anthony Wilden. Baltimore: Johns Hopkins Univ. Press, 1968.

LaPlanche, Jean. *Life and Death in Psychoanalysis*. Baltimore: Johns Hopkins Univ. Press, 1976.

Lejeune, Philippe. *On Autobiography*. Ed. Paul John Eakin. Trans. Katherine Leary. Minneapolis: Univ. of Minnesota Press, 1989.

Leppmann, Wolfgang. *Rilke: A Life*. Trans. Russell M. Stockman. New York: Fromm International Publishing, 1984.

Lindop, Grevel. *The Opium-Eater: A Life of Thomas De Quincey*. New York: Taplinger Publishing, 1981.

Lucian. *The Works of Lucian of Samosata*. Vol. 1 Trans. H. W. Fowler and F. G. Fowler. Oxford: Clarendon Press, 1905.

Luria, Alexander R. *Language and Cognition*. New York: John Wiley and Sons, 1982.

Luther, Martin. *Luther's Large Catechism*. Minneapolis: Augsburg Publishing, 1967.

Lyon, Judson S. *Thomas De Quincey*. New York: Twayne Publishers, 1969.

Lyotard, Jean-François. *The Post Modern Condition: A Report on Knowledge*. Trans. Geoff Bennington and Brian Massumi. Minneapolis: Univ. of Minnesota Press, 1984.

McGrath, F. C. "Joyce's *Portrait*." In *The Sensible Spirit: Walter Pater and the Modernist Paradigm*. Tampa: Univ. of South Florida Press, 1986.

Machiavelli, Niccolà. *The Discourses.* Ed. Bernard Crick. New York: Penguin Books, 1970.

Macmullen, Ramsay. "Two Types of Conversion to Early Christianity." *Vigiliae Christianae* 37 (1983): 175–98.

Mandel, Barrett J. "Full of Life Now." In *Autobiography: Essays Theoretical and Critical.* Ed. James Olney. Princeton: Princeton Univ. Press, 1980. 49–72.

Mazlish, Brude. "Autobiography and Psycho-Analysis." *Encounter* 35 (October 1970): 28–37.

Merleau Ponty, Maurice. "Eye and Mind." In *The Primacy of Perception.* Ed. John Wild. Chicago: Northwestern Univ. Press, 1964.

Montaigne, Michel de. "De Repentir." In *Essais de Michel de Montaigne.* Bibliothéque de la Pleiade. Ed. Albert Thibaudet. Paris: Gallimard, 1950.

——. "Of Repentance." In *The Essays of Montaigne.* New York: Modern Library, 1946.

Montefiore, Alan, ed. *Philosophy in France Today.* Cambridge: Cambridge Univ. Press, 1983.

Moore, Carlyle. "Sartor Resartus and the Problem of 'Carlyle's Conversion.'" *PMLA* 70.4 (September 1955): 679.

Morris, John N. *Versions of the Self: Studies in English Autobiography from John Bunyan to John Stuart Mill.* New York: Basic Books, 1966.

Morrison, Karl Frederick. *Conversion and Text: The Cases of Augustine of Hippo, Herman Judah, and Constantine Tsatsos.* Charlottesville: Univ. Press of Virginia, 1992.

——. *Understanding Conversion.* Charlottesville: Univ. Press of Virginia, 1992.

Murray, Gilbert, trans. *The Athenian Drama. Vol. 3. Euripedes.* London: George Allen, 1902.

Naumann, Helmut. *Malte Studien. Untersuchungen zur Aufbau und Aussagegehalt der "Aufzeichnungen des Malte Laurids Brigge" von Rainer Maria Rilke.* Reihe Deutsche und Vergleichende Literaturwissenschaft 7. Rheinfelden: Schäuble Verlag, 1983.

Nietzsche, Friederich. *The Use and Abuse of History.* Trans. Adrian Collins. Indianapolis: Bobbs-Merrill Educational Publishing, 1974.

Nock, Arthur Darby. *Conversion: The Old and the New in Religion from Alexander the Great to Augustine of Hippo.* London: Oxford Univ. Press, 1933.

Norton, M. D. Herter. Translator's Foreword. In *The Notebooks of Malte Laurids Brigge.* New York: Norton, 1949.

Olney, James. "Autobiography and the Cultural Movement." In *Autobiography: Essays Theoretical and Critical.* Ed. Olney. Princeton: Princeton Univ. Press, 1980. 3–27.

——. *Metaphors of Self: The Meaning of Autobiography.* Princeton: Princeton Univ. Press, 1972.

——. "Some Versions of Memory/Some Versions of Bios: The Ontology of Autobiography." In *Autobiography: Essays Theoretical and Critical.* Ed. Olney. Princeton: Princeton Univ. Press, 1980.

Palmer, Richard E. *Hermeneutics: Interpretation Theory in Schleiermacher, Dilthey, Heidegger, and Gadamer.* Chicago: Northwestern Univ. Press, 1969.

Pascal, Roy. "The Autobiographical Novel and the Autobiography." *Essays in Criticism* 9 (1959): 134–50.
——. *Design and Truth in Autobiography.* Cambridge: Harvard Univ. Press, 1960.
Peters, H. F. *Rainer Maria Rilke: Masks and the Man.* Seattle: Univ. of Washington Press, 1960.
Powell, Anthony. "George Orwell." *Atlantic Monthly.* October 1967.
Rank, Otto. *Psychology and the Soul.* Trans. William D. Turner. Philadelphia: Univ. of Pennsylvania Press, 1950.
Renza, Louis. "The Veto of the Imagination: A Theory of Autobiography." In *Autobiography: Essays Theoretical and Critical.* Ed. James Olney. Princeton: Princeton Univ. Press, 1980. 268–95.
Ricoeur, Paul. "Fatherhood: From Phantasm to Symbol." In *The Conflict of Interpretations: Essays in Hermeneutics.* Evanston, Ill.: Northwestern Univ. Press, 1974. 468–97.
Rilke, Rainer Maria. *Die Aufzeichnungen des Malte Laurids Brigge.* Frankfurt am Main: Insel Verlag, 1910.
——. *Briefe. Erster Band, 1897 bis 1914.* Wiesbaden: Insel Verlag, 1950.
——. *Briefe, 1907–1914.* Leipzig: Insel Verlag, 1931.
——. *Die Briefe an Gräfin Sizzo.* Leipzig: Insel Verlag, 1951.
——. *Briefe aus den Jahren 1914–1921.* Leipzig: Insel Verlag, 1937.
——. *Briefe aus Muzot, 1921–1926.* Leipzig: Insel Verlag, 1936.
——. *Journal of My Other Self.* Trans. M. D. Herter Norton and John Linton. New York: Norton, 1930.
——. *Letters of Rainer Maria Rilke, 1892–1910.* Trans. Jane Bannard Green and M. D. Herter Norton. New York: W. W. Norton, 1945.
——. *Letters to Marline, 1919–1922.* Trans. Violet M. McDonald. London: Methuen, 1951.
——. "Malte Laurids Brigge Prosa, 1906–1926." In *Sämtliche Werke.* Vol. 6. Ed. Rilke-Archiv, Ruth Sieber-Rilke. Frankfurt am Main: Insel Verlag, 1966.
——. *The Notebook of Malte Laurids Brigge.* Oxford: Oxford Univ. Press, 1984.
——. *Rainer Maria Rilke—Lou Andreas Salomé: Briefwechsel.* Wiesbaden: Insel Verlag, 1952.
——. *Selected Letters of Rainer Maria Rilke. 1902–1926.* Trans. R. F. C. Hull. London: Macmillan, 1946.
Rousseau, Jean-Jacques. *Les Confessions de Jean-Jacques Rousseau.* Book 3. Oeuvres Completes de Jean-Jacques Rousseau. Bibliothéque de la Pleiade. Paris: Gallimard, 1959.
——. *The Confessions of Jean Jacques Rousseau.* New York. Modern Library, 1945.
Sade, Donatien-Alphonse de. "Dialogue between a Priest and a Dying Man." In *The Marquis de Sade.* New York: Grove Press, 1965.
——. *Dialogue entre un prêtre et un moribond et autre opuscules.* Oeuvres Completes 7. Paris: Jean-Jacques Pauvert, 1961.
——. *The One Hundred Twenty Days of Sodom.* Trans. Austryn Wainhouse and Richard Seaver. New York: Grove Press, 1966.

Saldívar, Ramón. *Figural Language in the Novel: The Flowers of Speech from Cervantes to Joyce.* Princeton: Princeton Univ. Press, 1984.

SE = *The Standard Edition of the Complete Psychological Works of Sigmund Freud.* 24 vols. Ed. and trans. James Strachey. London: Hogarth Press and Institute of Psychoanalysis, 1953–74.

Seifert, Walter. *Das Epische Werk Rainer Maria Rilkes.* Bonn: Bouvier, 1969.

Shapiro, Stephen A. "The Dark Continent of Literature: Autobiography." *Comparative Literature Studies* 5 (1968): 421–54.

Shaw, Priscilla Washburn. *Rilke, Valéry, and Yeats: The Domain of the Self.* New Brunswick, N.J.: Rutgers Univ. Press, 1964.

Shumaker, W. *English Autobiography: Its Emergence, Materials, and Form.* Berkeley: Univ. of California Press, 1954.

Simenauer, Erich. *Rainer Maria Rilke: Legende und Mythos.* Bern: Verlag Paul Haupt, 1953.

Small, William. *Rilke. Kommentar zu den Aufzeichnungen des Malte Laurids Brigge.* Chapel Hill: Univ. of North Carolina Press, 1983.

Smyer, Richard I. *Primal Dream and Primal Crime: Orwell's Development as a Psychological Novelist.* Columbia: Univ. of Missouri Press, 1979.

Snoeck, André. *Confessions and Psychoanalysis.* Westminster, Md.: Newman Press, 1964.

Spender, Stephen. "Confessions and Autobiography." In *Autobiography: Essays Theoretical and Critical.* Ed. James Olney. Princeton: Princeton Univ. Press, 1980. 115–22.

Spengemann, William C. *The Forms of Autobiography: Episodes in the History of a Literary Genre.* New Haven: Yale Univ. Press, 1980.

Sprinker, Michael. "The End of Autobiography." In *Autobiography: Essays Theoretical and Critical.* Ed. James Olney. Princeton: Princeton Univ. Press, 1980. 321–42.

Stansky, Peter, ed. *On Nineteen Eighty-Four.* New York: W. H. Freeman, 1983.

Stansky, Peter, and William Abrahams. *Orwell: The Transformation.* London: Constable London, 1979.

Starobinski, Jean. "The Style of Autobiography." In *Autobiography: Essays Theoretical and Critical.* Ed. James Olney. Princeton: Princeton Univ. Press, 1980. 73–83.

Suleiman, Susan Rubin: *Authoritarian Fictions.* New York: Columbia Univ. Press, 1983.

Thornton, Weldon. *Allusions in Joyce's "Ulysses": An Annotated List.* Chapel Hill: Univ. of North Carolina Press, 1968.

Tillich, Paul. *Systematic Theology.* Chicago: Univ. of Chicago Press, 1957.

Turner, Victor. *The Ritual Process: Structure and Anti-Structure.* Ithaca: Cornell Univ. Press, 1969.

Underwood, Alfred Clair. *Conversion: Christian and Non-Christian.* London: George Allen and Unwin, 1925.

Vance, Eugene. "Augustine's 'Confessions' and the Grammar of Selfhood." *Genre* 6 (1973): 1–28.

Van Gennep, Arnold. *The Rites of Passage.* Chicago: Univ. of Chicago Press, 1960.

Wasson, Kirsten. "A Geography of Conversion: Dialogical Boundaries of Self in *The Promised Land*." In *Autobiography and Postmodernism*. Forthcoming. Univ. of Mass. Press.

Weinstein, Arnold. *Fictions of the Self: 1550–1800*. Princeton: Princeton Univ. Press, 1981.

Weintraub, Karl J. "Autobiography and Historical Consciousness." *Critical Inquiry* 1 (June 1975): 821–48.

Wilden, Anthony. "Lacan and the Discourse of the Other." In *Speech and Language in Psychoanalysis*. Baltimore: Johns Hopkins Univ. Press, 1968.

Woodcock, George. *The Crystal Spirit: A Study of George Orwell*. New York: Schocken Books, 1984.

Author Index